Outreach

Innovative Practices for Archives and Special Collections
Series Editor: Kate Theimer

This dynamic series is aimed at those working in archives and special collections as well as other cultural heritage organizations. It also provides students and faculty in archives, library, and public history graduate programs a resource for understanding the issues driving change in the field today.

Each book in the series tackles a different area in the field of archives and special collections librarianship and demonstrates the kinds of strategies archivists are using to meet these new challenges.

These innovative practices reflect approaches and ideas that will be new to many readers. The case studies featured in each book have been selected to keep in mind a broad spectrum of readers and enable the series, as a whole, to benefit a diverse audience.

Each book features case studies from both large and small organizations. Thus, some of the creative ideas presented are being implemented with costly tools and robust infrastructures, and others are being done on a shoestring. A hallmark of the series is that every case study incorporates ideas that are transferrable, even if the specific implementation might not be.

About the Series Editor

Kate Theimer is the author of the popular blog *ArchivesNext* and a frequent writer, speaker, and commentator on issues related to the future of archives. She is the author of *Web 2.0 Tools and Strategies for Archives and Local History Collections* and the editor of *A Different Kind of Web: New Connections between Archives and Our Users*, as well as having contributed chapters to *Many Happy Returns: Advocacy for Archives and Archivists, The Future of Archives and Recordkeeping* and the forthcoming *Encyclopedia of Archival Concepts, Principles, and Practices*. She has published articles in *The American Archivist* and the *Journal of Digital Humanities*.

Kate served on the Council of the Society of American Archivists from 2010 to 2013. Before starting her career as an independent writer and editor, she worked in the policy division of the National Archives and Records Administration in College Park, Maryland.

Titles in the Series

Outreach

Innovative Practices for Archives and Special Collections

Kate Theimer

ROWMAN & LITTLEFIELD
Lanham • Boulder • New York • Toronto • Plymouth, UK

Published by Rowman & Littlefield
4501 Forbes Boulevard, Suite 200, Lanham, Maryland 20706
www.rowman.com

10 Thornbury Road, Plymouth PL6 7PP, United Kingdom

British Library Cataloguing in Publication Information Available

Library of Congress Cataloging-in-Publication Data

Outreach / edited by Kate Theimer.
pages cm. -- (Innovative practices for archives and special collections ; 2) Includes bibliographical
references and index.
ISBN 978-0-8108-9097-8 (pbk. : alk. paper) -- ISBN 978-0-8108-9098-5 (ebook) 1. Archives--Public
relations. 2. Archives--Marketing. 3. Libraries--Special collections. 4. Library outreach programs. 5.
Archives--Public relations--Case studies. 6. Archives--Marketing--Case studies. 7. Libraries--Special
collections--Case studies. I. Theimer, Kate, 1966- editor of compilation.
CD971.O88 2014
025.1--dc23
2013049487

∞™ The paper used in this publication meets the minimum requirements of American
National Standard for Information Sciences Permanence of Paper for Printed Library
Materials, ANSI/NISO Z39.48-1992.

Printed in the United States of America

Contents

Introduction

The term "outreach" can describe a broad range of activities. For me, it means carrying out activities designed to inform potential users about a repository's collections and attract their interest in learning more about those collections. Over the past three decades, carrying out these kinds of activities, which include creating exhibits, conducting public programs, and publishing, has been an accepted part of the archivist's professional responsibilities. However, the importance of this function seems to have been consistently increasing in recent years. This rising interest has doubtless been triggered in part by the many new ways the web allows us to communicate with almost unlimited and unpredictable groups of people. But there are other probable causes, including greater competition for more limited funding and resources. Greater public awareness of archives results in greater potential public support for their work. A more positive source of inspiration for new outreach efforts is certainly also the desire among many in the profession to "open up" our repositories to new kinds of users who may not feel that they are welcome in an archives or special collections library.

Outreach, then, is an area in which one would expect to find many innovative practices, demonstrating creativity to interest new users in collections. With such a broad scope and no standards or rules constraining how or who to attract, archivists are limited only by their resources and imagination, although at times their organizations' tolerance for risk may come into play as well.

Outreach: Innovative Practices for Archives and Special Collections explores how archives of different sizes and types are reaching out to new potential users and increasing awareness of programs and collections. Some of the practices described in the case studies rely primarily on technology and the web to interact with the public, while others are centered on face-to-face activities. All of the case studies were selected because they demonstrate ideas that can be transferred into many other settings. This volume is useful to those working in archives and special collections as well as other cultural heritage organizations and provides ideas ranging from those that require long-term planning and coordination to those that could be immediately implemented. It also provides students and educators in archives, library, and public history graduate programs a resource for understanding the variety of ways people conduct outreach in the field today and the kinds of strategies archivists are using to attract new users to collections.

ABOUT THE INNOVATIVE PRACTICES SERIES

I debated with myself for some time over the title of this series, "Innovative Practices for Archives and Special Collections." After all, what is innovative and new to one person is often standard procedure to another. Another option was to call them *best practices* and follow the model of a series of similar books from the same publisher featuring case studies from libraries. But this seemed equally problematic. In a field that seems to embrace the phrase "it depends" as a mantra, putting forward the experience of any one archives as best practice seemed ill advised.

It is the very diversity of our field, though, that caused me to stick with my "innovative" label rather than shying away from it. There are new ideas in these books, or at least ideas that will be new to many readers. My philosophy in selecting case studies for the books in this series has been to keep in mind a broad spectrum of readers and to position the series so that it is as valuable as possible for a diverse audience. In each book are case studies from both big organizations and small ones. Some of the creative ideas presented are being implemented with costly tools and robust infrastructures, and others are being done on a shoestring. In determining what to include, I wanted to ensure that every case study incorporates ideas that are transferrable, even if the specific implementation might not be.

This commitment to making the series broadly valuable and practical has meant striving for a balance that favors more approachable innovations over implementations that are aggressively on the cutting edge. The ideas presented here are within the reach of most archives and special collections, if not right away, then in the near future. They represent the creativity and commitment to serving and expanding our audiences that I think are the defining characteristics of the archival profession in the early twenty-first century.

Because archival functions and processes are interrelated and don't always fit neatly into compartments and because most archivists perform several of them in the course of their daily work, the contents of each of the volumes in this series has both its own clear focus and overlapping relationships with the others. Case studies in reference and access touch inevitably on description and outreach. Because the overarching purpose of description is to facilitate use, issues relating to reference, access, and outreach are components of the case studies in that volume. The overlap of the management volume with all of the others should not be surprising, though the focus of the case studies there are more explicitly on management issues. These interrelationships are inevitable given the nature of archival work, and most practitioners and students will find all of the volumes useful.

Just as the activities archivists undertake depend on each other, so have I depended on the assistance of my friends and colleagues who generously agreed to review the case studies. My thanks to Rodney Carter, Amy Cooper Cary, Jim Gerencser, Mary Manning, and Tanya Zanish-Belcher for the time and careful consideration they have given to improving the books in this series.

ABOUT THE OUTREACH CASE STUDIES

Assessing innovation in outreach is a tricky issue, I think. Modern technologies aside, I suspect there is very little that is truly "new under the sun." But just because the concept of sponsoring things like contests, self-guided tours, volunteer opportunities, and open houses is not inherently original does not mean that specific implementations cannot find ways to innovate within the familiar. Therefore the case studies in this book provide both new ideas and twists on time-tested ones, some of them aided by new kinds of tools and technology.

Another consideration was how to define the book's scope. In response to the open call for case study proposals, I received a great many responses from archivists interested in writing about their instruction efforts aimed specifically at students. It quickly became clear that I could fill another whole book with case studies about instruction, and indeed that is what I decided to do. This series will continue to expand in the future, and a collection of case studies on instruction will be one of those future volumes.

One way of considering how to approach outreach, and so also the range of activities in this collection, is to ask:

- Who does the organization want to reach?
- How does the organization want to reach them?
- What is it that the organization wants to achieve?

While there are many ways of thinking about who an outreach activity reaches, for the case studies in this book, a useful method is to consider whether an activity is designed to reach a somewhat defined group of people, such as those who share a common interest or experience, or to connect with a wider—or undefined—range of people. Projects like the Oregon Archives Crawl, the Navigating Nightingale iPhone app, and the DIY History site are designed to appeal to people who want to make the effort to seek out opportunities to learn more about history. But they are also projects that weren't limited to people who had registered for a specific event or people who shared some kind of common background, as the continuing legal education classes at the University of Mississippi and the College of William & Mary's alumni projects were. A challenge for the National Archives at New York's Learning Center was to create a space for both kinds of outreach activities—both people who had signed up for a specific program and people who just wandered in to learn about history.

However, some of the most creative outreach efforts, and the ones with the most unpredictable results, weren't designed to appeal to any specific group of people—just those with an interest in something that might appear a bit unusual. The results reported here on the University of Manitoba's Hamilton séance video and the American Heritage Center's "Name the Tribble" contest illustrate the potential in this kind of audience under the right conditions. Similarly, the success of the Archives of American Art's collaboration with Wikipedia and the Library of Congress's resources on personal digital archiving is grounded on sharing specialized information with people who are actively looking for it. In all of these cases, the approach of the outreach activity was to put something out on the web and encourage people to interact with it to enhance their own lives.

In considering how an outreach activity reaches audiences, the most obvious consideration may be whether it takes place primarily or exclusively on the web or in person. In fact, one of the primary criteria in selecting case studies was to make sure there was a balance between those that described online-only activities and ones that were based on in-person interactions. While often it may seem that the web- or social media–based projects get the lion's share of the attention, there is no substitute for old-fashioned face-to-face activities, and this collection has representatives of both.

For example, in this volume Laura Stevens describes the success of the 21 Revolutions project at the Glasgow Women's Library in using its collections as inspirations for new works of art and literature and attracting audiences to gallery settings to connect with both the artworks and the inspirational sources. Those attending the continuing legal education sessions at the Modern Political Archives at the University of Mississippi, as described by Leigh McWhite, had more pragmatic aims in mind. But they, too, were exposed by their attendance to the perhaps unexpected value of archival collections—in this case the papers of Mississippi legal figures.

While in those projects the archival content was combined with activities that weren't focused on the archives, at the Oregon Archives Crawl, the archives were the main attraction. The crawl, aimed to get potential researchers inside the doors of not one but four archives as well as a brewpub. Amy Schindler's case study describes a similarly social atmosphere created around inviting alumni to visit the library to donate their time for a hands-on archival activity. Similarly, the experienced DC-area Wikipedians who joined Sara Snyder and her colleagues for a day of "behind the scenes" activity and information exchange at the Archives of American Art received a firsthand orientation to what archivists do and why. It was this behind-the-scenes atmosphere that Dorothy Dougherty and her team at the National Archives at New York City sought to re-create in designing the space for walk-in visitors to explore in the archives' new learning center.

Real-time interaction with archivists and other participants was critical to the experience created by all these outreach activities. In contrast, online or virtual outreach projects are designed to let people interact on their own time as their own interests dictate. The case studies contributed by Shelley Sweeney on the Hamilton Family Séance video, the University of Tennessee staff on sharing their images on social media sites, and Sara Snyder on expanding the Archives of American Art's inclusion in Wikipedia all describe manipulating information about collections and placing it on websites that people already love to visit: YouTube, Historypin, Pinterest, and Wikipedia. In this way they take advantage of being able to meet new potential users where they are. In the same vein, the Navigating Nightingale iPhone app created by King's College London is designed to literally meet users where they are by making archival materials the basis for a location-based walking tour app.

Other online outreach efforts capitalize on users' interests rather than where they are—either virtually or physically. Rachael Dreyer's creative "Name the Tribble" contest attracted *Star Trek* fans from around the country and the world. The success at the University of Iowa in attracting people interested in the Civil War to their site to transcribe handwritten documents led to the development of the larger and more sophisticated DIY History site. While at Iowa the archives wanted its users to help them, the goal of the Library of Congress's personal digital archiving web presence is to help people manage their own digitally created collections.

In addition to thinking about with whom and how outreach activities are designed to work, another way to analyze them is to consider what they are designed to achieve. In most cases the goal of outreach activities is multifaceted. Archivists and special collections librarians want to encourage use of collections, increase visitation (either online or in person), raise general awareness of the collections, and encourage donations. They may also want to achieve goals related to advocacy, such as defining or reinforcing the role the archives plays in the community and encouraging support for funding.

While all outreach efforts share these general goals, some efforts are designed with a specific result in mind. Although the "Name the Tribble" contest didn't have a predetermined audience in mind, it did have a specific endpoint: the selection of a winning name for the tribble. The 21 Revolutions project also had a concrete purpose: the creation of twenty-one new works of art and twenty-one new works of literature. The purpose of the DIY History site and its predecessor, as described by Jen

Wolfe and Nicole Saylor, was to generate transcriptions of historical materials (as well as to engage people with the documents themselves). The various alumni volunteer projects related to the archival materials of the choral program at the College of William & Mary were very concrete and pragmatic. The alumni who attended these events felt a sense of accomplishment in doing something to contribute to the preservation and access of archival collections. Outreach that features educational programs, such as those described in the case studies from the University of Mississippi and the National Archives at New York, are also results oriented. All attendees should leave those programs having achieved preidentified learning outcomes. Events are planned, executed, and evaluated. While they may be part of ongoing programs, they have distinct beginning and end points.

In contrast, outreach projects like the Hamilton YouTube video, the University of Tennessee's use of Historypin and Pinterest, the AAA on Wikipedia, the Navigating Nightingale app, and the Library of Congress's personal digital archiving resources are more open ended. The products they generated continue to be discovered and used after the "event" of posting them is completed. In a larger sense, however, that is true of all successful outreach activities. Their impact continues to be felt even after the event or activity has concluded.

While each case study in this collection describes a specific approach to reaching new audiences, I think each also reflects a philosophy of experimentation that is perhaps the most crucial ingredient for any organization interested in developing its own "innovative" practices. In this regard I hope this book and the others in the series encourage all readers to consider how their own work could benefit from the exploration of new ideas and tools. The books in this series can, by definition, include only a small sample of the kinds of approaches being developed by archives and special collections around the world to meet the challenges of staying relevant and adaptable in today's complex environment. These case studies give readers many useful ideas to consider, as well as the inspiration to come up with tomorrow's innovations.

ONE

The Oregon Archives Crawl

Engaging New Users and Advocates

Diana Banning, Mary B. Hansen, and Anne LeVant
Prahl, Portland Area Archivists

In 2010 the Portland Area Archivists launched the Oregon Archives Crawl to connect a broader, atypical audience with the resources of the large and small archival institutions in Oregon. The event originated out of our desire to broaden community awareness, interest, and access to archives. During a time when the region was at risk of losing major institutions, we realized the fate of Oregon's archives might very well rest not only on our ability to increase our user base but also more importantly build awareness among people unfamiliar with archives as a cultural resource. The more people we engage with our collections, the better they will appreciate our mission and gain an understanding of the value our institutions bring to the community. A public who is aware of the importance of archives is in a position to advocate for and become users of our collections. Our own interconnectedness as colleagues provided new avenues for getting that message across. And that is where our story begins.

We imagined an event at which anyone interested in or even curious about archives and history could easily learn about a majority of the area archives without needing to travel far. We chose downtown Portland as a central place for the event. Luckily there are four archival institutions within a ten-block area: City of Portland Archives and Records Center; the Portland State University Special Collections and University Archives; Multnomah County Library; and the Oregon Historical Society.

These host institutions became the destination locations for our "archives crawlers" (who became known as "crawlers", for short) to visit. At the host locations, representatives from the following thirty-six regional archives and heritage organizations staffed tables and talked to crawlers about their own collections (see textbox 1.1).

The crawl ran from 10:00 a.m. until 4:00 p.m. on a Saturday. Crawlers began their day at any of the four host locations. After picking up a map and receiving an orientation about the goals of the day, they visited with archivists, viewed materials on display at the various tables, attended special programs, or took a tour before moving on to the next host location. Programming varied at each location, as did times for facility tours of the host institutions.

To encourage people to visit all four locations, we created a "passport" that also served as a directory of area archives and heritage organizations. Filling the passport with stamps from each host location entitled a crawler to be entered into a drawing for prizes donated by many of the host and participating organizations. At the after-party, which started just as the crawl portion closed, prizes were handed out, thank-you speeches were made, and the conversations that had begun during the crawl around the participant tables could continue. A slide show full of images submitted by each institution ran in the background while beer was consumed (far away from archival documents), and elevator speeches were replaced with socializing. For three years the day of the Oregon Archives Crawl has been a way to connect people with archives and archivist with archivist, both helping us to build a strong foundation within the community.

PLANNING

Collegial connections made the Oregon Archives Crawl possible. For many years, the Portland Area Archivists have met regularly over lunch. Our group has no formal organization, bylaws, or membership requirements. We maintain an e-mail list of anyone interested in the group, and our noon gatherings are open to everyone. We bring a bag lunch to a different venue within a fifty-mile radius of Portland and sit around a table with fifteen or twenty people who all do roughly the same job and swap ideas. We never create an agenda in advance, nor do we take minutes. It is social time that culminates with a tour of the archives that is hosting us that month. This communion of colleagues has resulted in impromptu mentoring situations, the sharing of important information about incoming collections and upcoming projects, and the placement of interns into situations that best suit their needs. Sometimes during these chaotic conversations, a comment made can plant a seed for future collaboration.

Architectural Heritage Center
Association of Personal Historians
Century of Action Committee
City of Portland Archives and Records Center
Dill Pickle Club
Episcopal Diocese of Oregon
Genealogical Forum of Oregon Library
Hellenic-American Cultural Center
Lewis and Clark College Watzek Library
Mazamas Archives & Museum
Multnomah County Library
Metro Records & Information Management Program
Multnomah County Records Management & Archives
Northwest History Network
Oregon Black Pioneers
Oregon Cultural Trust
Oregon Encyclopedia
Oregon Health & Science University Archives
Oregon Historical Society
Oregon Jewish Museum
Oregon Maritime Museum
Oregon Nikkei Legacy Center
Oregon Public Broadcasting
Oregon Shakespeare Festival
Oregon State Archives
Oregon State Library
Oregon State University Special Collections and Archives
Pacific University Library
Portland Art Museum Library
Portland Police Historical Society
Portland State University Special Collections and University Archives
University of Oregon (Portland)
Washington County Heritage Online
Washington County Museum
Western Oregon University
Willamette University Archives

Textbox 1.1. List of participating institutions

In 2009, a half dozen of us were packed into a van, returning from a grim discussion with our colleagues in Salem, Oregon's capitol, about dwindling budgets and the future of heritage institutions. You would think our mood would have been gloomy, but the tone for this congenial group of friends and colleagues was lively and even hopeful. We brainstormed ways to have the people of Oregon connect with its archives. We envisioned bringing new people into the archives to see us in a new light, to know more and care more about the resources available to them. Thus the idea for the Oregon Archives Crawl was born.

Perhaps it says something about those of us who happened to be in that van, or perhaps it says something about Portland itself, that the concept of transforming the traditional pub crawl into a marketing tool for archives awareness was an instant hit. Portland is the self-proclaimed microbrew capital of the country, and pubs are everywhere. There are open taps at a local swimsuit store, and down the street from there is a brewpub/bicycle repair shop combination. We saw our opportunity to give archives the same kind of whimsical presence, even if only for one day. We took our cue from the McMenamins brewpubs, which collaborate with the Oregon Historical Society and the Holy Names Heritage Center to organize monthly "history pubs" on topics of local interest. If McMenamins can serve the public both beer and education about history at the same time, we reasoned, then so can we. In comparison to other statewide efforts to build excitement around the concept of preserving documents, we thought this one stood out.

Many of the past attempts to mark Archives Month in Oregon have resulted more in serving the professional archives community than in reaching the visiting public. Symposia with interesting speakers, film screenings, and the like tend to attract those for whom archives are already well understood. Other programming—a day at one of McMenamins's historic properties and an "Antiques Road Show"–style day of expert advice—was also attended largely by our regular patrons and visitors. There was discussion among us about whether events hosted by archives could draw people who were not already supporters or patrons. Many of us believed that the problem wasn't that our audience was finite but that our approach so far had been directed toward the "usual suspects," reaching out again and again to those who already supported archives. The archives crawl concept had the potential to achieve our goal of getting hundreds of new faces through our doors. We wanted to bring our archives to the streets, so to speak. Instead of focusing on our current audience, we'd find a way to entice people who had never set foot in an archives into visiting not just one but multiple archives. The goal was not necessarily to create instant researchers but to raise awareness of the existence and purpose of archives and the abundant local heritage resources. Before the van had arrived back in Portland, we were brainstorming a list of archives to invite.

We sent out inquiries to the Portland Area Archivists' e-mail list to ask for volunteers to help create and plan an archives crawl event for Archives Month. We knew a good plan is nothing without a good committee to see it through. Our first meeting in January 2010 laid the groundwork for all subsequent planning. We determined the structure of the crawl, with four host institutions and participant tables and a passport for crawlers to carry with them from one location to the next. We decided to host an after-party where we could all relax, reflect, and debrief with the crawlers when it was over. We formalized a list of organizations in the region to solicit for participation. Based on these general ideas, we divided into subcommittees and started our to-do lists.

The steering committee met monthly for about nine months prior to each archives crawl and with increased frequency as the date of the event approached. There we generated new ideas, provided updates to each other, and got motivated to keep the ball rolling. Meeting in person helped us brainstorm ideas for additional organizations to approach and provided personal contact that kept us on task. We agreed on the language we would use in our press releases, and we voted on poster designs. We also found our meetings to be a path to fostering other collaborations and strengthening the network of local archives.

We realized that an essential part of our meetings was a reliable note taker. Brief and bulleted minutes of each meeting, with decisions that were reached and action items that had been agreed upon, kept us all on the same page and gave us a framework to act within. It was also effective to assign the action items generated at each meeting to a specific person or committee and to create a deadline. Because we came to the table as colleagues with a long history of sharing our work lives with each other, we had a common understanding of the kinds of time constraints and administrative pressures we each were juggling. We knew that with so many moving parts and a committee made up of volunteers, identifying discreet tasks and naming a person who was responsible for them and a time they needed to be completed was crucial.

A volunteer note taker sent minutes out via e-mail and posted them to the Google Group created for the Portland Area Archivists. Using Google Groups provided us with a virtual space to disseminate information; update our list of participating organizations; and draft press releases, posters, and other promotional materials. Having a shared online space helped keep each of our individual efforts on track and allowed us to include members who were not able to meet in person. Our documentation from year to year helped us improve our process and streamline our efforts.

The first order of business was to set the date for the event—not an easy task. Saturday was selected as our best opportunity for bringing in the maximum number of people, although this meant a lot of archivists would be working on what would normally be their day off. Because the plan was to include the crawl as part of celebrating Oregon Archives Month, we were limited to the Saturdays in October. We also had to work around religious holidays and competing events at some of our participating institutions. Lastly, we had to find a Saturday when space would be available for the after-party we were also planning. Eventually all of the pieces fit together; we had our four host venues, we had a place for our after-party, and we finalized a date.

Once we got organized, defined our goals, and chose a date, the next step was to introduce the archives crawl concept to our colleagues at archives and heritage organizations in our region and invite them to participate. We all agreed that we needed to be inclusive in our efforts and reach out to as many local organizations as we could. To help encourage participation, we used the professional connections of all of the committee members and professional organizations to discover smaller institutions that might have escaped our awareness. Our goal was to cast a wide net, including inviting organizations that may not keep collections of their own but still promote interest in the field. We created a list of forty to fifty possible participants and handed it over to a committee to make the contacts.

We sent a letter by mail to our institutional colleagues to introduce the idea of the archives crawl and to let them know that we would be contacting them. Before a week had passed, we followed up the letters with a personal phone call to each institution and then a follow-up e-mail with more information about how to sign up. Follow-up e-mails and phone calls helped solidify participation and generate enthusiasm. They also proved instrumental in making sure that we were reaching the right person within each institution—a person who could make the decision about whether they would staff a table.

The key to our success in corraling up to thirty participating organizations each year was a detailed spreadsheet including contact information, notes about conversations, and details about the status of various deadlines, including passport information and images for the after-party slide show. It was extremely helpful to have a single point of contact for all of the participating organizations, ensuring that the correct information was distributed and tracked to each of the organizations. This spreadsheet was the foundation for our efforts in the following years.

The archives crawl transformed in each of its three consecutive years, and not surprisingly, each year presented its own set of challenges. Planning in the first year was intense because we were creating something out of nothing and all ideas had to be sifted and evaluated. Subsequent years became easier because the groundwork we had already laid was in place and we had a successful event behind us. We continued to float new ideas each year, however, always eager to build on that success and expand our scope. This ambition to offer more each year was not accompanied by a new wave of volunteer power or a sudden influx of funding. We were constantly reminding ourselves at planning meetings to plan within our means in terms of money, time, and energy.

One place where we learned to plan within our means was creating and executing the after-party. We were caught off guard by how difficult that turned out to be. We wanted beer to be part of the event (we were planning this in Portland, Oregon, after all) but were limited because most of the host institutions were government bodies and most government agencies have a prohibition on alcohol in their buildings. The after-party seemed like a perfect way to wrap up the event and provide a way for the participants who had been separated among the four host venues to discuss how the day had gone. The public would be encouraged to join us and talk shop. The first year the after-party was held at one of the four host venues. We offered live music and raffle prizes (donated by local history-minded businesses) and assumed that everyone would have a great time.

Suffice it to say that the planning committee opted to have the after-party off site in later years. McMenamins Pubs was happy to have us come to them rather than donating the food and beverages. This relieved us of all but the simplest planning for the party. The pub provided a band again the second year and waived the minimum purchase fee for using their venue. While we didn't receive direct confirmation from McMenamins, based on the amount of food, beer, and spirits that were purchased by the after-party attendees, we suspect that we were a money-making event rather than a donation. This was generally heralded as an improvement to the original plan.

IMPLEMENTATION

From maintaining contact with participating organizations to marketing, creating, and placing signage, setting up the four host venues, and throwing an after-party, the implementation of our many planning efforts required careful coordination. Once we had a list of the organizations that had agree to participate, the planning committee began dividing the participants among the host institutions, according to available space for them because each host had varying amounts of space to offer. We chose to separate like organizations as much as possible, creating an even balance at each host venue of government archives, university collections, historical societies, and community history organizations. At this point communication between the participants and the crawl could be turned over to a representative from each of the host institutions. The hosts could better answer specific questions about the table arrangements, availability of Wi-Fi, lighting, projectors, and other needs the participants might have. They could also answer the ubiquitous question we had not initially anticipated: Is parking available?

Because we were committed to including a list of participants in our promotional materials, the marketing efforts could not begin in earnest until the majority of the participating organizations had committed to staffing tables. With the four host venues established and the participating tables assigned, implementing a marketing strategy had to become our priority. Acting on all of our well-conceived plans required all of the resources we as volunteers could muster. It was immediately clear that the planning committee did not have the energy, money, or skills to carry out all of our plans alone. We would have to recruit, beg, and borrow. Help came in the form of volunteer time (which we solicited from colleagues and local archives students), nominal funding, and free online resources. Cash funding consisted of fifty-dollar grants from the Northwest Archivists (our regional archival association), which helped defray such costs as paying for a bartender, other refreshments, and shipping bags that the Society of American Archivists (SAA) donated. The remaining support came from institutions donating materials or directly paying for specific things like signs and fliers. For some of the participating organizations, the planning efforts were seen as part of their yearly outreach efforts. This allowed those committee members to complete their tasks during work time and to donate resources. Others had to put the time in as volunteers outside of their regular work hours.

The most notable in-kind donation was the artwork for the event poster (see figure 1.1). A local graphic designer has volunteered his skills and time each year to create a poster design for us. The benefits of professional work on our graphics cannot be overstated. Suddenly the event had a presence we could market to our colleagues and to the public. We used the poster designs on the archives crawl website and in other free online promotions. The printing of the passports as well as the posters was another in-kind donation from within the host institutions that we could not have done without. The poster and passport are good examples of how we were able to execute a large-scale event without an event budget. When the design and printing were completed, a host of volunteers came together to spend an afternoon folding and assembling the 500 passports.

The completion of the design meant that we now had something we could announce to the public. We utilized a variety of online resources, including social media and our own event website. Having little to no funding, we identified as many free resources as possible to promote the day. We created a Wordpress blog to host our event website (http://pdxarchivists.wordpress.com). The participating organizations each used their own social media outlets to push the message further. We created a Facebook event and encouraged all of our committee members and participants to invite their Facebook friends. From there, visitors were again directed back to the crawl website for further details. On Twitter we created a hashtag (#archivescrawl), and one volunteer took on the task of putting out short teasers once a week for a month to keep interest up. The event website remained the place with up-to-date crawl information; all other media outlets were asked to redirect traffic to that site. This system

Figure 1.1. Poster art for Oregon Archives Crawl 2011, created by Sean Garrison

produced a consistent message and gave our web volunteers just one site to maintain.

Most of the participating organizations already had outreach tools in place with a base of their supporters and followers. These newsletters, e-mail lists, Twitter feeds, Facebook pages, and institutional blogs were invaluable to us as a method of letting the public know what we were doing. A cross-pollination effect occurred so that a person who may be a regular on the list of one participating archives became a brand new audience for another. Connecting all of the archives and heritage organizations broadened the appeal and allowed us to reach more people.

Beyond the supporters from each of our individual media lists, we discovered we were reaching new groups of people that we would never have had access to before. Our Facebook posts and tweets about the archives crawl and related activities took on a life of their own as our followers reposted and retweeted to their own followings. We learned that many of these people were not associated with any of our participating organizations. We did a search for web mentions about the crawl after the fact and found buzz about the event we had not driven, including a Meetup group formed to attend the crawl together and praise as being the "highlighted event of the weekend" by bloggers to whom we had not pitched directly.

Each year our marketing efforts have expanded. In the third year, we worked with two locally owned theaters that offer beer and second-run movies; these theaters agreed to display our advertisement as part of their premovie slide show. The theaters were chosen because they catered to a younger demographic, they supported local business, and they were willing to try something new. In short, their patrons were not the usual suspects when it comes to archives-related events.

We sent committee members and volunteers out to distribute fliers at the local farmers' markets and public arts events. The second archives crawl coincided with the height of the Occupy movement, and one archivist walked through the Occupy Portland camp handing out fliers. We also piggybacked on media interest in the Oregon Archives Month itself. We had the government archives among us pass proclamations focusing on the statewide celebration. Because many news agencies follow their local governments for news stories, this power of association proved useful. That publicity inevitably drew attention to what we were doing in Portland.

As the day drew closer, signage for each of the four venues was created, printed, and distributed. All participating organizations were reminded to use their networks to continue to get the word out: newsletters, press contacts, social media, institutional communications, and community outreach all combined to create excitement about the day.

The day of the archives crawl dawned early for those participating. About an hour before the public was expected, participants with boxes of material arrived to set up. These early hours provided an opportunity for us to make use of the many archives students who had volunteered to help. The campus of Portland State University is host to an enormous farmers' market on Saturday mornings, and coincidentally two of our four host venues were also on the university campus. We took advantage of the crowd of shoppers by sending volunteers with signs and fliers out among the shoppers to encouraging them to join the crawl when they had finished purchasing vegetables. This seemed to have been successful given the number of crawlers we spotted with shopping bags sporting greens.

Predicting the ebb and flow of the crowds proved difficult because we had no idea how many people would show up. Crawlers were often waiting at the doors before the start time, eager to begin the crawl and to tour the host venue. These tours of the host facilities turned out to be a crowd favorite. People appreciated getting behind-the-scenes tours and did not mind if they had to wait until the next tour started. They indicated in exit surveys that this was a highlight of the day. Participating organizations were also encouraged to incorporate an activity at their table, and many complied while also displaying unique and unusual materials. By the third year, we had created a committee to facilitate additional programming, such as viewings of short films and panel discussions on local history. Each of the four host venues set aside an area where archivists could present on a topic or provide mini-workshops.

In addition to talking with people at the crawl and asking for their feedback, we wanted to capture their responses in a measurable way. To gauge the impact of the event on crawlers, each venue distributed written surveys to be filled out on site. We also solicited online feedback by printing a link to the survey on the back of the passport.

RESULTS

In its most important aspect, we have succeeded in meeting the objective we had in mind when we envisioned the archives crawl: We reached new audiences with our message. Each year we averaged between 250 and 300 crawlers, with a large percentage of them new to the crawl and new to archives. Most venues had surges of crawlers come through, but there was always a steady pace throughout the five-hour day. One venue that gave many tours during the day informally polled all of their tour groups and found that nearly 30 percent of the attendees had never before visited an archives. This percentage was corroborated by our paper and online surveys.

While most people responding to the survey, either on paper or online, had compliments to share, they also had suggestions that we used to improve the following year's crawl, such as lowering the music volume at the after-party and improving signage. We also sent a survey to the participating organizations about their experience staffing tables. We received many responses to this survey, and all of the responding organizations rated the crawl as being a "good" or "excellent" outreach tool, with most indicating that it was excellent.

As shown from our informal poll and from our own conversations with the attendees, the Oregon Archives Crawl achieved the desired results each year that we produced it. We wanted to draw in people who would not normally attend an archives event, we wanted to bring together a critical mass of archives, we wanted the event to be a collaboration between colleagues, and we wanted to make it fun. How did we know it was fun? The comments people made on the survey supported the feedback we received from the crawlers and participants the day of the crawl. For example, some of the answers we received to the question "What was your favorite part of the Crawl?" were:

- I liked being able to see the historical items, documents, and photographs in person instead of through a textbook or the Internet.
- Meeting people and sharing stories.
- Great info tables from so many area institutions. This event is a great opportunity for some small/little-known institutions to connect with the public.
- The pictures. The wide variety of histories represented, and learning so much about Portland history. I liked going to different buildings.
- Getting to go behind the scenes.
- As we were walking here, we heard an "Occupy Portland" protester making a speech calling out congress and the banks. Here I saw the leaflets and photos of workers protesting the reduction of jobs and unemployment relief in 1935. It's good to see ties to our past.
- Learning that all these resources exist!

In response to "Will you attend the crawl again next year?" we got answers like: "Yes, I love letters, photos. I mean to visit museums. Events like this actually get me here." and "Maybe. I know where to go now and may just come on my own."

Of course not all feedback was glowing; people had many ideas on how to make it better. However, not one person indicated they had a terrible time or that they would not attend another crawl.

An interesting measure of the crawl's success was the attention it gained from our colleagues across the country. We fielded inquiries from several organizations asking about the event and how we planned it. We presented the concept and our approach at the Northwest Archivists' annual meeting. Based on later Archives Month activity reporting, it appears at least a few of these organizations adapted the concept for their own version of the Oregon Archives Crawl.

Another gauge of the event's effectiveness came much after the fact; archivists would report that first-time researchers came into their facility mentioning that they'd been to the crawl.

LESSONS LEARNED

The first archives crawl was an experiment. We learned from our successes and our missteps. Our success in bringing in large numbers of attendees gave us the confidence to seek new audiences for the subsequent years. Our experience with organizing the after-party taught us to seek out the expertise of others.

While respondents suggested more programming each year, very few of the participating organizations found they had the time or staff to provide programming in addition to planning a table display. Also the flow of the crowd from one venue to another didn't always lend itself to planned programming because people were on different time tables and started at different places. The greatest success came from the host organizations that provided talks, mini-workshops, and other activities. In retrospect, trying to have the participating organizations come up with programs required more planning and logistical considerations than it merited. This is a case where we learned the limitations of volunteer efforts.

Another case in which we learned to impose limitations was in the level of involvement we expected from the participating organizations. In the crawl's first year, we offered each organization the option of sending us their brochures and other written material in lieu of staffing a table of their own. This idea turned out to be a drain on our planning committee's time and was very little utilized by the crawlers, who had come for the day prepared to engage in conversation with us, not to collect our literature. The "literature only" table was rejected for subsequent years.

In other areas we learned we needed to expand our efforts instead of limit them. Each year we received feedback about frustrations surrounding our signage: not enough, not in the right places, too small. With this in mind, we tried to standardize the signage formats, solicit input for where the signage should go, and create a comprehensive list of what signs were needed. Even in our third year and with all of the planning, we were still scrambling at the last minute to get signs in place.

Some of the lessons we learned were not things we could solve. The planning committee members often found that they were spending so much time organizing the whole event that the logistics for their own repository's participation was left to the last minute. Those working the day of the event had little chance to break away to use the restroom or take a lunch break, let alone time to visit the other venues. Many of the archivists found it ironic that the organizers never experienced the crawl to its fullest extent and missed seeing what each of the other organizations had to offer. The fatigue of being on for so many hours and talking with so many people meant that many participants went home after the crawl was over and never made it to the after-party. Those who did were very ready for a drink! Although we acknowledged this problem every year, we understood that it was necessary to provide the best experience for the public.

The biggest lesson we learned was acknowledging our limitations as party organizers. The after-party is an essential component of the event. It is also the area in which we have made the most adjustments from year to year. The first year's after-party took an inordinate amount of the committee's time to plan and execute and did not go as smoothly as we would have liked. Based on our experience and the copious feedback we received after the first after-party event, we took steps to improve the planning and the event for the following years.

We had solicited raffle prizes from the participating organizations and awarded them to winners drawn from among the crawlers who had successfully collected passport stamps from all four host venues. Among these prizes were photo books, historic photographs, buttons, free memberships, and other promotional swag from many of the organizations. We learned after the first year that grouping the items into two to three large prizes is far easier to facilitate, especially when the winners are not present to pick up their prizes. Two to three large prizes also increases excitement and decreases the amount of time it takes to draw the winning names.

The selection of music was another area that provided learning opportunities. We wanted fun music at the after-party to draw in people, especially young people. And while the bands were fun and very lively, the feedback we received was that the music was too loud and people were unable to talk over the music. Learning that the draw of the after-party was more about conversation than dancing, we opted in the third year to provide a playlist of local music that would play in the background at a level that allowed conversation.

CONCLUSION

If the goal of outreach is to sow the seeds of awareness and hope that they grow into interest and eventually into advocacy, then the crawl was widely successful for the organizations that participated and for archives and special collections everywhere in the area. New audiences continued to appear each year. We did not seem to be reaching a saturation point among members of the curious public. The lighthearted tone of the event is partially responsible for that. All four of the venues worked to dispel the stereotype of the profession as stuffy and boring. This was a day to be having fun with what we do. The archivists staffing tables kept up lively conversations, laughed as they answered questions, and generally promoted an atmosphere of good fun.

In the wake of our success, it was a difficult decision to suspend the archives crawl for the time being. After three years of intense planning, the steering committee no longer had the energy to begin the process for a fourth time. In the third year, a plea went out to all of the past participants asking for more support, including requesting that all institutions commit to participating on one committee. We had varying success with our attempts to distribute the workload, but still these efforts did little to change the reality that a very small group of people did the majority of the work. Because the crawl was so popular, we had hoped that a new steering committee would be created to take over for the departing committee, but unfortunately new leadership did not emerge.

This decision does not take away from the success of the event, however, which still provides an outreach model for future efforts. The connections between archival institutions allowed the Oregon Archives Crawl to thrive. And those connections remain strong and amiable. As archives adapt to new realities, archivists are exploring new ways to connect to each other and our patrons and to reach out to new populations. Archives can not exist in silos. The Portland Area Archivists believe that the Oregon Archives Crawl created an environment for forging new connections and strengthening the place of archives within the region.

Diana Banning is the city archivist for the city of Portland, Oregon. Mary B. Hansen is the assistant archivist at the city of Portland Archives and Records Center. Anne LeVant Prahl is the curator of collections at the Oregon Jewish Museum.

TWO

Moved by the Spirit

*Opportunistic Promotion of the
Hamilton Family Séance Collection*

Shelley Sweeney, University of Manitoba

The Hamilton Family fonds documents the investigations into life after death conducted by Doctor Thomas Glendenning (TG) Hamilton and his wife Lillian just after the turn of the last century in Winnipeg, Canada. The séance photos in particular are so astonishing, so powerful, that they literally induce a visceral reaction in many viewers. They certainly made the hair stand up on the back of my neck the first time I saw them, having just assumed my position as head of the University of Manitoba Archives & Special Collections in the fall of 1998. I decided then and there to let as many people know about the collection as possible. My first consideration was what kind of outreach we should do.

One way to do outreach is the deliberative approach employing extensive consultation, thoughtful analysis, careful planning, and strategic evaluation. Then there's the improvised type of outreach that relies on a gut appreciation of worth combined with a scattershot adoption of new systems and technologies as they develop, the layering of outreach opportunities one atop another, and the exploitation of available individual talents when they become apparent. Promotion of the Hamilton Family fonds has relied heavily on this latter approach to outreach, coupled with an enthusiastic embracing of the unconventional with a dash of hearty disregard for potential controversy.

A number of new technologies were employed as they became available, but probably the single most important tool in publicizing this collection was the creation in 2008 of a YouTube video of séance photos. The video is just over four minutes long and features thirty-five still images from the collection integrated into a constantly moving tableau, accompanied by oddly stirring but distinctly eerie music. We did not know exactly what to expect when we posted the video, but it succeeded beyond our wildest dreams in capturing the imagination of the public and provoking a strong reaction. The response to our previous attempts at outreach coupled with the video has gone well beyond raw numbers of hits, views, likes, and comments to cause a virtual explosion of popular and scholarly use of the materials in ways totally unimaginable before the Internet. Given my original intent to make as many people aware of the collection as possible, our outreach efforts, however unplanned and perhaps at times downright chaotic, have certainly been a success. While it would be impossible to recreate our steps, there are some broader lessons to be drawn from our experience about how first to recognize and seize opportunities as they arise and second to match the opportunity with the right individual's abilities.

The Hamilton Family fonds specifically documents the inquiry into life after death by TG Hamilton, his wife Lillian, and daughter Margaret from 1920 until TG's death in 1935 and by Lillian and Margaret from 1935 to 1944. The investigations began shortly after the death of the Hamiltons' three-year-old twin son, Arthur, who died unexpectedly in 1919 during the influenza epidemic and who was said by Margaret to have sparked the family's interest in the possibility of an afterlife. The Hamiltons conducted their investigations through the use of mediums in séances or "home circles" (see figure 2.1). Hamilton House on Henderson Highway became a center for spiritualist activities and scientific investigation.

Although TG was well known for his career and public life as a medical doctor, member of the Manitoba legislature, elder of his church, and so on, it was the family's spiritualist activities that made them famous throughout Canada, the United States, Britain, and beyond. From 1926 to 1935, TG gave eighty-six lectures throughout North America and overseas and wrote numerous articles on psychical investigation that were widely published. The family, in turn, was visited by some of the leading spiritualists and mediums of the day, including British author Sir Arthur Conan Doyle; famous Boston medium Mina "Margery" Crandon and her husband, Dr. R. L. G. Crandon; Hungarian-born British and American psychologist Nandor Fodor; and Canadian prime minister William Lyon McKenzie King.

Most of the photographs show mediums and sitters in trance states. The early photographs mostly focus on telekinesis, or the movement of objects by the mind, whereas the later photos feature a ghostly medium called *ectoplasm*, often containing faces or in the shape of people or objects (see figure 2.2).

Figure 2.1.   A wide-angle photograph of the medium, Mary Marshall, with the so-called umbrella "ectoplasm" enveloping her head during a séance at the home of Dr. Thomas Glendenning Hamilton on February 25, 1934. Hamilton Family fonds, Group XV, #55 - "Umbrella" Teleplasm, First Exposure (Wide Angle) UM_pc012_A79-041_010_0008_055_0001

Additionally these paranormal investigations included rappings, clairvoyance, trance charts, wax molds, bell ringing, transcripts, and visions. The graphic material, including photographs, glass plate negatives and positives, prints, slides, and scrapbooks of photos, are undoubtedly the most popular part of the collection. To a much lesser extent, the textual materials also garner attention and include séance attendance records and registers, affidavits, automatic writings, correspondence, speeches and lectures, news clippings, journal articles, books, tapes, manuscripts, and promotional materials related to major publications. The textual material mostly appeals to scholars and enthusiasts. This part of the fonds has not been exploited nearly as much as it should be given the amazing range and depth of documentation that exists.

One issue that often arises is the veracity of the contents of the materials, particularly the photographs. Are they real, or are they fake? To us their value does not lie in their truthfulness. Their value lies in their reflection of social concerns after the First World War and the 1918 flu epidemic. The photos themselves, as far we can tell, are an authentic

Figure 2.2. Medium Mary Marshall releases ectoplasm featuring the face of Sir Arthur Conan Doyle during the séance held May 1, 1932. Doyle had died in July of 1930. Hamilton Family fonds, Group XII, #44a - First Doyle, First Exposure (Enlargement) UM_pc012_A79-041_010_0005_044_0002

representation of what went on in that room at Hamilton House; according to various photographic experts, the photographs and negatives have not been altered. Whether fraudulent activities occurred in the room and by whom they were perpetrated are different questions best answered by scholars.

PLANNING

As early as 1997, the archives under Dr. Richard Bennett had fashioned a simple website that featured the finding aid for the Hamilton papers in two separate places. A student hired before I arrived at the university had created a small virtual exhibit on agriculture using his personal scanner at home. That encouraged the archives to purchase one of the first scanners on campus, which allowed us to scan further images from our collections to mount on the Internet. I began hunting around and got a small internal university grant to hire another student. The intent was for the student to create seven small virtual exhibits on diverse subjects based on our most valuable and high-profile archives. One of our summer masters of archival studies interns had expressed an interest in learning how to scan archival materials and upload them to the Internet. Once I had obtained the grant and hired the student for the project, she duly taught herself all the skills needed to create virtual exhibits. As it turned out, she was unable to finish the project in the time required but was able to teach another student, Brett Lougheed, who eventually became our digital archivist, so he could complete the project for her by creating a website on spiritualism. He used eight startling photos from the Hamilton family collection. By early 2001 all the exhibits were mounted on the Internet.

Although small and relatively primitive by today's standards, anecdotally we can point to this spiritualism exhibit as the beginning of wider international attention for the fonds: One of the curators for "The Perfect Medium" exhibit held in 2004 at the Maison Européenne de la Photographie, Paris, and the Metropolitan Museum of Art, New York, phoned me to ask about the collection, stating that his research assistant had found it through this virtual exhibit online. Notwithstanding this elevated profile, not all attention to this collection at this early time came from the Internet. One local professor from our sister university, the University of Winnipeg, likes to tell the tale that she was searching for spirit photographs at various archives in Paris only to have staff at one institution tell her to have a look at the famous collection at the University of Manitoba!

This was the beginning of our journey to expose the séance collection to a wider audience. Three staff members, including Brett, were successful in applying for a provincial heritage grant in 2005 for a small amount of money to digitize unique images in the fonds. Of the total 2,681 photos, only 760 are unique; all the other photos are duplicates in various formats. The most complete view of a particular shot was selected from among duplicates in the collection, digitized at a resolution of 600 DPI, and saved as TIFF files to a local server for preservation purposes.[1] Low-resolution access copies were derived from these masters to create an online collection. Each image was described utilizing the Dublin Core metadata schema. This metadata was then indexed and made keyword searchable on the website. There was a relatively brief delay until Luna, our new image management system, was brought online, however the Hamilton photos were ingested in October 2006 and were then available to the public on the web. When I returned from my sabbatical in January 2007, we officially launched the online collection.

Response to the photos was immediate and very positive. Stories appeared in a variety of specialized online sites, including *Our Strange World* and *Paranormal Review*, as well as more traditional news and university websites. Unfortunately, our IT people had difficulties providing statistics from the Luna image management system, so we were not able to reliably track the website's use for any length of time. We did get one year's worth of data (2007–2008) for accessing individual photos: 18,183 hits. However, due to incompatibilities in the infrastructure, Luna began to crash, first on an irregular basis, then more and more frequently, forcing us to search for a replacement system. During this time, then, even if we were able to track uses, the statistics would have been gravely impacted by the instability of the system.

Following this digitization project, one of our most dedicated researchers into the Hamilton Family fonds secured a Hamilton travel grant to come to our repository to work directly with the materials and offered to give a lecture during his visit. We scheduled his lecture for September 11, 2003, the second anniversary after the 9/11 terrorist attacks. This was entirely coincidental; it just happened to be the week that the speaker was in town, and Thursdays are our preferred day of the week to hold lectures as it seems to garner the largest audiences. However I believe the anniversary date definitely contributed to the response to the event. Instead of 25 to 30 people turning up the evening of the lecture, 255 people came out, necessitating a sudden change in venue. One might speculate that the lecture on life after death was more attractive at the time because of people's worries about the suddenly very real possibility of death. We have since held two more lectures on various aspects of the Hamilton family without nearly the same response.

But all of these projects were mere preludes to the project that had and continues to have the greatest impact on the popularity and knowledge of the fonds, and that was the creation of our YouTube video. While these run-up projects did not constitute planning per se, they had the effect of testing the waters to see what the response might be to further promotion. And the digitization of all unique images was a particularly important building block for all future promotion of this collection.

IMPLEMENTATION

The pièce de résistance of all of these attempts to publicize the Hamilton séance collection was the YouTube video produced in January 2008. My awareness of the value of the site for outreach was triggered when a colleague at another institution forwarded me a link to a video of my hometown soon after the video was uploaded to YouTube in December 2006. I was very impressed with the combination of still archival photos and evocative music. I contacted the poster, who turned out to be an amateur enthusiast of archival photos. I asked him how he cleared the copyright for the music (which was a commercial production), and he replied that it was not an issue. Later on I returned to the video and found the music had been blocked by the copyright holders, so indeed it did turn out to be an issue, although the music was eventually restored through an agreement.

Inspired by this apparently relatively simple approach to creating a video, I picked out some photos from our *Winnipeg Tribune* newspaper collection with the hope of putting together something equally catchy. In March 2007 a member of the library technology department tried to create a basic video from these photographs as a proof of concept, employing Moviemaker, a simple video editing program available as part of the Microsoft suite. The results were tantalizing but not very satisfying. However, this sample video had two important results: It proved that a video could be made relatively quickly and easily, and on seeing the video, it led the manager of digital library planning and development to suggest that the Hamilton séance photos were more suited to the quirky contents typically being posted to YouTube at that time. The demo video also indicated that, for a satisfying result, the project would require someone who had a specific talent for and/or experience in making videos.

It seemed so obvious once the manager made the suggestion that Hamilton should be the subject of the video and fit perfectly with my desire to promote the collection. With the content of the video now decided, the next issue was to find appropriate music. I picked out music that had been very effectively used by the local office of our public broadcaster, the Canadian Broadcasting Corporation (CBC), for a brief television spot on the Hamilton collection. I was not successful however in finding out how I could buy the rights to that music; even though staff at the station tried to be helpful, they worked through companies that bundle music that CBC purchases. I then spent many hours on the Internet looking for appropriate and free music but felt myself defeated. Having experienced how important the music was to my reaction to the original video of archival images on my hometown, I knew that having the right music was crucial to the end product. And given the offbeat content of the Hamilton video, the music had to be equally compelling.

At the same time, serendipitously, an off-site researcher needed a local student to do research for him on some of our other archives for a documentary he was developing. As no masters of archival studies students were available, we hired Robert Ross, a former teaching assistant (TA) in film studies. He was so good that, when he had finished his research contract, we hired him to work on other projects. Meanwhile, an internal university grant for another outreach project actually came in slightly under budget, leaving a few weeks' worth of money that allowed us to hire Robert to work on the YouTube video.

It was a perfect storm: We had an archival fonds that had material perfectly suited to be mounted onto YouTube; YouTube was still quite fresh and in particular hadn't been saturated with videos based on historic archives; we had some extra funds that could be broadly used for outreach; and we had a graduate student who was both willing and capable of working on the project.[2] In addition, he had an excellent relationship with the film studies department, so he was able to return to use their sound studio and all of their high-end film software to make the video. He also knew both a film instructor and a lab technician who were able to provide technical support when he was using the equipment. The most important aspect, and one that we couldn't have predicted ahead of time, was that he had an excellent inherent talent for both making videos and composing music in addition to his top-notch work ethic that allowed him to complete the project in a very short period of time.

Because the unique photographs were already online, it was an easy enough task for me to select startling images to be used in the video, which then Robert could add to as needed. I had the sample of music from CBC that Robert could listen to, and I gave him a pretty good description of what I wanted. His first rough cut of the video wasn't quite what I had in mind, but further discussion between us resulted in small adjustments being made. He then composed and recorded the music. The final cut of the video only required a bit of tweaking of the text, adding some explanations at the bottom of a few of the photos (i.e., "levitation" and "teleplasm/ectoplasm"), and providing our URL at the end, and we were good to go.

The video starts with this text in silence: "In 1918, Dr. TG Hamilton of Winnipeg, Canada, began researching the paranormal through séances and mediums."[3] A few seconds later, this text is joined by: "The following authentic photographs were taken by Dr. Hamilton over the course of his investigations." These two texts set the scene for the photos that follow. The ominous music starts just as the photos begin. The photos are presented in a variety of ways. Sometimes the camera pans across a photo or briefly lights upon it and then cuts to another photo, zooming into details, moving in and out, sometimes fading to black, with other photos fading into each other. This movement is extremely effective, as is the accompanying music. The final shot is the bank of eleven cameras Hamilton used to record the images, followed by the credits, which identify that the photos came from the Hamilton Family Photograph Collection at the University of Manitoba. We eschewed the use of the word *fonds* as being too confusing. The video ends with the URL for the archival description, which had links to the finding aid, the digitized material, and back to the YouTube video.

A day after the video was posted to the Internet, the University Public Affairs Office issued a news release. The story also was posted on the front page of the university's website.

RESULTS

There are two ways, I think, to talk about the impact of the YouTube video: First, review the hard data about the video itself, and second, discuss the increase in the overall use of and prominence of the Hamilton collection.

The immediate result of the posting of the video was a flood of media attention: The story was featured on national nightly news-hour television; it aired on a national cable TV station; it was covered by one of the local newspapers; and it captured an impressive center spread in one of our national newspapers, something virtually unheard of for a university story and meriting a mention by the vice president (external) during a senate meeting! The video made the list of the top YouTube videos in the education category. Searching the web after the video was uploaded, I found that it had spread the fame of the Hamilton Family fonds far and wide; I was able to find information about the video and the fonds on websites as far away as Japan, Brazil, and France.

Since its posting, the video, although not "viral," has been viewed nearly 250,000 times at the time of this writing, with more than 270 likes, 70 dislikes, and a whopping 789 comments. The number of people viewing the original video was given an enormous boost within three days of being posted by a plug on an American night-time talk radio show devoted to "strange occurrences, life after death, and other unexplained . . . phenomena" called *Coast to Coast*.[4] This syndicated radio show airs on more than 560 stations in the United States, Canada, Mexico, and Guam, with nearly 3 million weekly listeners. It regularly devotes episodes to such themes as "Theories of Atlantis" and "Alien Contact and End Times," so the Hamilton video was entirely in keeping with their profile.

Since the launch of the video, however, the number of visits has remained pretty steady, averaging about 2,400 per month. Nearly a year after the video was posted, we also uploaded it to our own channel, which had been developed by then. This version has also had a steady although much more modest clientele, with nearly 7,000 views in total. Another viewer reposted our video with a brief French commentary at the beginning, for another 9,000-plus views. Neither of these later versions has generated many likes, dislikes, or comments.

I think we can say, then, that the video itself has been a success in terms of sheer numbers, although we cannot say for certain how many people were inspired by it to look at our website or the finding aid for the collection. However, what we can say is that the sheer range and volume of projects that have incorporated the Hamilton Family séance photographs since the launch of the video is astonishing. Can all of these be directly attributable to the video or even the placement of the materials and descriptions on the Internet? Probably, because there has been such an upswing in use since these projects were launched. In any case, my goal of raising the profile of the collection and bringing it to the attention of the public using whatever means we had at our disposal has been achieved.

Our success may also be due in part to a concomitant increase in scholarly interest in spirit photography and early paranormal movements, but again most of these scholars likely find the collection online. Thus, if we had not been actively promoting our materials, interested scholars might not have found them. A number of academics, graduate students, and art historians studying the belief systems of spiritualism, the development of modern alternative religions, and the struggle to blend religion and science in the modern period have incorporated the fonds into their work. Scholarly books, articles, theses, and symposia on spirit communication, the effects of the 1918 influenza epidemic, and the use of women as mediums have also been based on this collection. One of the most recent uses of the fonds has been by a graduate student exploring cultural history employing digital fabrication and physical computing tools, which, in the case of the Hamilton photos, essentially turn two-dimensional photographs into three-dimensional images.[5]

The Hamilton Family fonds also has held great appeal for private individuals and organizations interested in the paranormal. There are Internet biographies, YouTube videos, and paranormal websites that feature the Hamilton séance photos. For example, an individual in Canada spent five years transcribing all of the Hamiltons' handwritten notes.[6] These transcriptions were then translated into Spanish by another individual in Spain on the site *SurvivalAfterDeath/CienciasPsiquicas*.[7] There are nearly 300,000 hits on Google for the name *Thomas Glendenning Hamilton* alone that show him featured on a wide variety of sites in multiple languages. If one uses alternate versions of his name in connection to the paranormal, the number of hits rises to over a million. TG even has his own independent Facebook page! Much of the current interest is from people who believe or want to be persuaded that there is scientific proof of spirits.

Perhaps the most unpredictable influence of the fonds, however, has been as an inspiration for cultural objects: plays, novels, television shows, art exhibitions, videos, and films. Carolyn Gray wrote the play *The Elm Street Visitation* in 2007, which was then published as a book.[8] Christina Penner followed with *Widows of Hamilton House: A Novel* in 2008.[9] Television shows have included everything from episodes on the *Creepy Canada* series to the very popular American series *Fact or Faked: Paranormal Files* and more.[10] Art exhibitions including both original and reproduced photos from the Hamilton Family fonds have been shown in such varied locations as Stockholm, Paris, and New York. A performance art piece by A. A. Bronson and Peter Hobbs featuring Hamilton photos and others in a queer context was performed in five locations in Canada and the United States and resulted in the book *Queer Spirits* in 2011.

Photos and documents from the fonds have been featured in everything from the American commercial horror film *The Haunting in Connecticut* (2009) to the Brazilian autobiography *A Suprema Felicidade* (2011) by Eduardo Pagnoncelli to the mysterious and enigmatic video installation *F-L-A-M-M-A-R-I-O-N* (2009) by Northern Irish artist Susan MacWilliam.[11] *F-L-A-M-M-A-R-I-O-N* was one of three installations for MacWilliam's solo exhibition "Remote Viewing" at the fifty-third Venice Biennale in Italy in 2009. The Biennale is considered to be the largest art show in the world, with an attendance of more than 300,000 visitors, so the profile of this piece was very high. Further, after the show, MacWilliam took *F-L-A-M-M-A-R-I-O-N* to the Republic of Ireland, Northern Ireland, and a number of cities in Canada, and she published a book from the installation.[12] A local film by auteur filmmaker Guy Maddin entitled *My Winnipeg* (2007) featured the Hamilton family and used the photos as an inspiration for a further scene.[13] The film was a critical success, named by Robert Ebert as one of the top ten films of the decade.

Finally, our efforts to promote the Hamilton Family fonds have not stopped at the YouTube video. We used grant funds in 2008 to hire Robert Ross once more to scan and describe 1,344 pages of séance notes, which were also ingested into Luna. We had colleagues translate the fonds' description into French, Polish, German, and Japanese. We continue to give lectures and speeches and radio and television interviews to whomever shows the slightest interest. This includes speaking to such varied groups as Creative Retirement Manitoba and the Humanists, Atheists, and Agnostics of Manitoba.

LESSONS LEARNED

In a case like this, the institutional context you are working within is very important. For our project, there were two ways in which this contributed to our success: first in our ability to explore and use new technologies relatively easily and second in our ability to highlight a collection with at least some potential for controversy. We are fortunate to have an amazingly supportive and nonbureaucratic structure at the University of Manitoba Libraries, but our casual approach to promotion would not work in an institutional setting less inclined to embrace new technologies (which YouTube was at the time) or that had a rigid attitude toward procedures and approvals. The only negative feedback we got about our use of technology was from a member of the libraries' technology team who tried to discourage us from posting to YouTube as he was worried that we were providing a for-profit company rights to do whatever they wanted with the video. The only negative feedback we got about our choice of content came from a man who phoned to say that he thought we were bringing shame to the university and to the city. His tone was deeply conservative. In the end, after I indicated that we had the highest support of the university (which by that point we did), he had to back off. Otherwise all other staff who commented on the video were deeply enthusiastic. But that certainly might not have been the case in some other settings, so knowing your institution's tolerance for risk is critical.

Another factor in our success was the role played by our university public affairs department. They had the expertise and contacts to be able to publicize our efforts in the most effective way. It is always better to tap into such expertise within your own institution. They in turn depended upon me to be available and to communicate with enthusiasm why the media should be interested in this promotion. It is always best to only have staff who are both comfortable and knowledgeable speak to the media. It is no good to have a representative of the highest level of your unit speak to the media if they are unfamiliar with the material.

However, despite our excellent relations with our public affairs department, or perhaps because of them, the department did cause us a bit of trouble. Because I was so excited about the video, I made the mistake of telling our university public affairs staff person about it before we were ready to launch. He rushed us into production, and this was a mistake. The student had typed in our URL instead of copying it and made an error. When the public affairs staff pointed this out to us, the student changed it immediately and reloaded the video only to discover that reloading gave the video a totally new address, different from the one sent out in the news release. And because we really did not know much about posting videos at the time, even though YouTube was already over a year old, Robert Ross posted it to his own personal account. So we had a bit of an issue with the URL, which could have been avoided if we'd had more time to post and test it without the pressure of an outside deadline. When we finally established our own channel for the archives later on in 2008, we posted the video, but it was of course given an address different from the video posted to the student's account, and so our stats are not cumulative. After, the URL at the end of the video leading viewers to the archival description of the fonds was succeeded by a new address, so even though the old pages still came up when searched (thank you Internet!), some of the internal links to other pages had been cut. This was easily rectified but had not been considered after the video was succeeded by other promotions and our website upgraded. It is wise to keep a list of all external projects to ensure that all links both to and from them are changed when any home website changes occur.

In addition to public affairs' own extensive list of media outlets, over the years the archives had built up mailing lists of persons interested in the paranormal or the history of the paranormal. We sent out notices about the YouTube video to all those on our list. Particularly in the days before Facebook and Twitter, these lists were crucial to reaching specialized audiences. Even today we still rely heavily on this personal communication. Those we communicate with usually are quick to pass on the word to others with similar interests.

Then there were a number of lessons that we learned about working with YouTube that can apply to any Web 2.0 projects in which you interact with the public. We were trying to be clever by using the word *authentic* at the beginning of the commentary to our video. The photos are authentic, but many commenters understood the word to mean that the contents of the photographs were real, which was not something we were claiming. This has led to a lively exchange between those who either believe the contents are real or who would like to believe that they are real and those who emphatically believe they are fake. Of those in the latter camp, there are some who believe the photographs have been Photoshopped. This could mean that they did not watch the video to the end or did not read the credits saying that this film was produced from archival sources or that they do not realize what an archives is and what one might expect from an archives, that is, not Photoshopped photos. I was astonished at the visual illiteracy of some of the commenters. There were people who were not even aware of the relative age of the photos. They could not draw any conclusions from either what the people were wearing or the look of the photographs. The unusual nature of the contents of the photographs also spurred many joking comments.

I participated in the discussion a fair bit at the beginning to try to clarify matters, but this did not last. I gave up because my replies did not seem to make a dent in the type of negative comments that appeared, that is, people clearly did not read earlier comments before making essentially the same remarks over and over. I also gave up because I did not have the time to keep track of comments or queries that could benefit from a useful answer. This exchange from 2011 is typical of some of my responses:

> Commenter: @BrandonIsWinning they were remade it was proven.

> Me: This is the Archives speaking. These are our photos. They were not remade. These are original photographs taken between 1919 and 1945ish. I'm not saying anything about the contents, but I can validate that the negatives were not tampered with. i.e. if there were fraud, it was not the photographer.

> Commenter: you can tell there [sic] straight up staged. just look at it

> Me: Yes, but you are talking about what people were doing in the room, not the photographs themselves. It wouldn't take much to evade the controls the Hamiltons had placed on the mediums, to smuggle stuff in, for example. Not that I'm saying that's what happened, just that we know the photos themselves hadn't been altered. A television company brought in a professional photographer who examined the plate glass negatives and he says there was no tampering with the negatives.

While for us this kind of debate and confusion was intensely interesting, for a more sensitive or risk-averse organization, this might be a very serious issue. I think the approach we took—not emphasizing at the outset the "archival" nature of the photos or spending time explaining their context—helped contribute to the popularity of the video. But some, although certainly not all, of the misunderstandings about what the photos represented might have been avoided if we'd taken a more didactic tack.

Although the total number of comments pales in comparison to popular ghost and UFO videos on the Internet, the comments are more numerous than archival material normally elicits. The question is whether this type of engagement is useful, particularly if the commenters do not understand that these are archival photographs from a reputable institution. I would argue that you need to start the popular promotion of archives somewhere and that everyone who views these photos does take something valuable away from the viewing that will perhaps be the basis for new lessons learned in other contexts.

My concern about getting the music right was validated: Judging from the comments, the music seems to be a significant component of the video. The music, combined with the so-called Ken Burns effect of panning and zooming on still images, has the interesting effect of concentrating one's eyes on specific details, details that are lost when one glances at the entire image at once.[14] I believe that, without the music or with music that was not nearly as effective, we would not be getting such sustained interactions with the photos.

The timing of the release of the YouTube video at the time when the university was developing its own roster of digital offerings was important. Both the university and the media were hungry for appropriate digital content. Today there is more competition for attention, but good-quality digital material is still sought as now organizations must feed websites, Facebook pages, Twitter feeds, and so on.

As I've noted, part of what enabled us to succeed was our staffing. In every part of the evolution of our outreach efforts, we were able to use the talents of individual students who were not full-time staff members. This allowed us to do far more than the amount of money available to us warranted both because each student could bring his or her own unique talents to the project and because, being paid more modestly, they could work longer on the projects for the amount of money we had. Even if we had more funds, however, the projects would still be dependent on finding the right fit of individuals with the proper talents for the job. We were lucky that the people with the right skills came along when we already had a project in mind. Now that we have the position of digital archivist dedicated to investigating digital technologies that might be appropriate for the archives, we do not have to rely on the incidental talents of casual students. By having the masters of archival studies program at the University of Manitoba, however, we regularly have new students complete internships with us every summer, so this lets us explore other avenues of promotion with them. We also more recently have had the ability to use volunteers who bring a variety of distinct talents for promotion with them. Having this range of talents supports the kind of "opportunistic" outreach that we've used to promote this collection.

CONCLUSION

The successful promotion of the Hamilton Family fonds has led us to acquire new fonds relating to psychical research and the paranormal, to develop an occasional lecture series and yearly newsletter on this topic, to acquire the top-notch advice and assistance of a number of dedicated and highly knowledgeable volunteers, and to expand our efforts into international fund-raising. Thus, a simple desire to promote a significant fonds has developed into a full-blown archival program.

In the future we will continue to develop this area of acquisition and to create such outreach tools as opportunities arise. The various activities in promoting the Hamilton Family fonds have not been systematically planned and evaluated, but they have been iterative. It is true that our promotion could be done in a more measured and calculated fashion, but we really do not have the staff complement or the time to invest too heavily in these activities. And our iterative approach also gives us some advantages. If we try a promotion and it does not work as well as we expect or would like but we have not invested a lot of time or effort in it, then we have not lost anything. If the promotion does work well, then we use it as a learning experience.

We do want to more carefully and regularly monitor our statistics through Google Analytics, which we are anticipating being able to do with our new digital asset management system. In the meantime we have one more possibility for getting the Hamilton Family fonds listed on the UNESCO Memory of the World Register, which was rejected in 2013 despite our best efforts. This would be very appealing to our paranormal believers and would give a major boost to the fonds' popularity among that fan base and with our primary funder, the provincial government. We will also continue to consider the Hamilton Family fonds or any of the other paranormal fonds for any new methods of outreach that come along as the spirit moves us.

Shelley Sweeney, Ph.D., is the head of the University of Manitoba Archives & Special Collections, The Libraries.

NOTES

The author would like to thank colleagues Brian Hubner and Brett Lougheed and former staff member Robert Ross for their assistance in writing this case study.

1. This is a bit problematic, as the most complete shots are not necessarily the vintage shots, that is, those printed by Hamilton at the time of the taking. We had not had the vintage prints identified at that point, something that was later achieved by another student from the Ryerson University masters in photographic preservation and collections management interning at the Hudson's Bay Company Archives in Winnipeg.

2. The copyright for the fonds was transferred to the university upon donation, however all the photos were in the public domain by the time we used them in the film, so copyright was not an issue for us.

3. "TG Hamilton's Photos of Ectoplasm," YouTube video, 4:06, posted by manitobaclays, February 27, 2008, accessed October 15, 2013, http://www.youtube.com/watch?v=W0HncGNBCqY.

4. *Coast to Coast AM,* accessed October 20, 2013, http://www.coasttocoastam.com.

5. Devon Elliot, "Sense of Depth," *Devonelliot.net,* September 9, 2013, http://devonelliott.net/2013/09/09/sense-of-depth.

6. Walter Falk, *The T. G. Hamilton Files,* accessed October 15, 2013, http://www.thehamiltonfiles.info.

7. "Los Archivos de TG Hamilton," *SurvivalAfterDeath/CienciasPsiquicas,* accessed October 26, 2013, http://survivalafterdeath.blogspot.ca/2011/07/los-archivos-t-g-hamilton.html.

8. Carolyn Gray, *The Elm Street Visitation* (Winnipeg, MB: Scirocco Drama, 2007).

9. Christina Penner, *Widows of Hamilton House: A Novel* (Winnipeg, MB: Enfield and Wizenty, 2008).

10. "The Hamilton Archives," *Creepy Canada,* OLN (20032004); "Raining UFOs/Ectoplasmic Pic," *Fact or Faked: Paranormal Files,* SyFy (2011).

11. Peter Cornwell, *The Haunting in Connecticut* (Beverley Hills: Gold Circle Films/Lionsate, 2009). This film features a portion of twelve photos and employed the entire

fonds as research, particularly about ectoplasm; Eduardo Pagnoncelli, *A Suprema Felicidade*, (Brazil, Ramalho Filmes); Susan MacWilliam, *F-L-A-M-M-A-R-I-O-N* (2009).

12. Susan MacWilliam, *Remote Viewing* (London: Black Dog, 2008).

13. Guy Maddin, *My Winnipeg* (Winnipeg, MB: Buffalo Gal Pictures, 2007).

14. Interestingly, Ken Burns credits a 1957 Canadian documentary, *City of Gold*, with inspiring his panning and zooming technique. *City of Gold* was directed by Colin Low and Wolf Koenig, http://en.wikipedia.org/wiki/Colin_Low_(filmmaker).

THREE

Working within the Law

Public Programming and Continuing Education

Leigh McWhite, University of Mississippi

While archivists commonly attend conferences and seminars to acquire knowledge within their own field, few have considered the possibility that participation in another profession's continuing education program may serve as a valuable mode for outreach. Participation in continuing education programs enables repositories to attain several important goals. In addition to encouraging large audience turnouts, these events raise awareness of the archives among a targeted population of professionals, enhance a repository's profile with an institution's high-ranking administrators, and please collection donors.

Continuing education (also known as "continuing professional development" or "continuing professional education") is a structured means by which members of a profession seek to improve and update their knowledge and skills after formal training concludes. Courses, workshops, and seminars are offered by state and national associations as well as nonprofit and for-profit providers. In some locales an association or licensing board may actually require a certain level of continuing education each year. Examples of professions that commonly mandate continuing education include accountants, health care providers, financial managers, teachers, and lawyers.[1]

This case study examines the efforts of the Modern Political Archives at the University of Mississippi to promote awareness of law-related collections among the state's legal community through coordination with the university's Center for Continuing Legal Education. While focused on the law, the approach described is easily adapted to other fields with similar accreditation requirements.[2]

PLANNING

Established in 1854, the law school at the University of Mississippi (UM) is the fourth-oldest state-supported school of law in the United States.[3] It is one of only two law schools in Mississippi and the only one at a public institution. As a result, an overwhelming amount of the state's practicing attorneys received their degrees from UM. Similarly, a large number of the state's judges and politicians are also alumni. These facts explain why the law school has received several important donations of congressional, judicial, and legal collections over the last forty years.

Unfortunately, despite the eagerness of the law school to acquire these donations, it provided no resources for processing the collections and making them available to researchers. The papers essentially languished untouched and unused in storage until 2004, when the administration transferred responsibility for more than 7,000 linear feet of collections to the Department of Archives and Special Collections. The department then created the Modern Political Archives (MPA) as a new unit combining the collections transferred from the law school with previously existing political and legal papers in special collections. Today, MPA holdings total approximately 12,500 linear feet.[4]

MPA operations during its first four years concentrated on the consolidation of its holdings into a newly renovated facility and the processing of congressional and other political collections. However, by 2009 MPA began to devote a small percentage of staff hours toward the papers of Armis Hawkins, a former chief justice of the Mississippi Supreme Court. The records management practices of judges and the nature of the content are distinct from most other collections typically held at a nongovernmental repository, and developing processing guidelines required some research because these were the first set of judicial papers handled by the archives.[5] Although a peripheral project in the greater workload of MPA, the Hawkins papers still represented a considerable investment in labor. When completed in 2010, the significance and scope of the collection demanded some form of promotion.[6] A program to commemorate the life of Chief Justice Hawkins and the opening of his collection seemed like the perfect choice to spearhead the publicity. Because MPA held a number of other judicial papers in backlog, Hawkins would serve as the inauguration of a law-related archival series highlighting these various collections over the coming years.

Archives and special collections have organized many public programs in the past, and despite good planning and promotion, the turnout has sometimes proved disappointing. Planning an event is a serious commitment of time and energy. Special collections has only seven full-time employees and no designated outreach personnel. Rather, each curator and archivist tends to take the initiative for promoting the holdings in his or her area of responsibility. With other duties looming, it is simply not an efficient use of resources to arrange a program that fails to achieve an audience.

For special collections, a program attended by thirty or more is considered a success. The largest gathering for a departmental event occurred at a noontime brown-bag program in September 2008 entitled "Tell Every President to Listen to the Blues." Featuring the blues archivist and a radio show host discussing presidents mentioned in blues lyrics, the program coincided with the 2008 presidential debate of candidates Barack Obama and John McCain on the campus of the University of Mississippi. More than one hundred people packed into the room. Why such a large turnout? Students attending officially sponsored debate activities and programs such as this one received stamps in a passport. Each stamp increased that student's chances in a lottery distributing tickets to the presidential debate.

Yet another event during the debate demonstrated the important role incentives can play in drawing a crowd to the archives. An earlier brown-bag program featured women's political collections, and included among the panelists was the president of the state division of the League of Women Voters. During the planning process, she asked if her organization could use the department's space afterward to host a program on judicial election versus judicial appointment. The archives readily agreed. Approximately seventy individuals attended that event, mostly lawyers drawn by the prospect of earning continuing legal education (CLE) credit hours.

The turnout made a definite impression. Two years later, when planning began for the Armis Hawkins program, it seemed obvious that CLE accreditation would allow MPA to target a specific external professional audience with a clear interest in the subject matter.[7] To explore the possibility, consultations took place with the CLE administrator on campus about accreditation approval. The process proved surprisingly easy. The state Commission on Continuing Legal Education has granted presumptive credit approval for programs sponsored by UM's Center for Continuing Legal Education. After discussing the planned program, the campus administrator approved one hour of credit for those attending the Hawkins event.

In Mississippi, practicing attorneys must attend or complete a minimum of twelve hours of CLE programming or course work each year. In a few states, CLE is optional. It is fairly common for institutions with law schools to operate a CLE department. Usually it is under the administrative umbrella of the law school, but in the case of UM, CLE is a part of the Division of Outreach and Continuing Education.[8] If the university had

lacked a CLE department, I would have had to apply directly to Mississippi's authorizing commission and allowed several months for a reply.

In Mississippi and elsewhere, these commissions typically post online
their standards for gaining accreditation approval, and they all tend to
follow a similar script. In reviewing my state's protocols, I discovered
that the activity must be open to all licensed attorneys in the state (although if seating is limited, registration is acceptable). The event's sponsor (in this case the university) must have a demonstrated ability to organize legal training or legal education, and the coordinator should have
qualified practical or academic experience. As to content, the primary
objective of the activity should be "to increase the participant's professional competence as an attorney" and to cover material "related to the
practice of law and the professional responsibility or ethical obligations
of attorneys." In addition, the program must feature a moderator as well
as a question-and-answer session, and participants should receive a well-
prepared handout. To offer one hour of accreditation, the event must last
a minimum of sixty minutes. On the administrative side, the sponsor
must verify and report attorney attendance to the commission in a timely
fashion. Participants must also have an opportunity to complete an evaluation questionnaire on the program, and the organizer must forward a
summary of the results to the commission.[9]

I thought it prudent to line up at least three main speakers for each
program, as occasionally speakers have dropped out at the last minute. In
addition to providing some cushion in case of an unforeseen absence,
most people are happy to participate if informed that they need only
prepare a fifteen-minute address. With greetings and introductions by
the moderator, this format still leaves ten to five minutes for a Q-and-A
session at the end.

At times, programs about a single individual (like a judge) can end up
as purely laudatory tributes to the honoree. Some of this is unavoidable
and also not entirely to be rejected. Such accolades are natural and greatly appreciated by the family, friends, and colleagues present. However,
to obtain CLE approval, I made a concerted effort to include at least one
scholar in each panel. Speakers also received a fairly focused description
of what their address should cover. For example, former law clerks are a
natural resource for programs on specific judges. With these individuals,
MPA requested that they discuss the work habits of the judge (How did
he handle the caseload? What was the process for writing opinions? What
was he like in court?). For the Hawkins program, MPA asked a highly
respected lawyer and close friend of the donor to conduct a countdown
of the top ten most significant judicial opinions written by the former
chief justice. Another close friend and federal judge provided a biographical account. I also participated in that panel, describing the preservation,
processing, and historic value of judicial papers in general and the Hawkins collection in particular.

In the second CLE program on the judicial papers of J. P. Coleman (former chief judge of the U.S. Court of Appeals for the Fifth Circuit), a current member of that bench with a strong interest in the history of the court described Coleman's nomination and confirmation process. A former law clerk reminisced about his mentor, and a political science professor discussed the administrative realignment of the Fifth Circuit during Coleman's tenure as chief judge. As moderator for the event, I used my welcoming remarks to outline the mission of the repository and describe the historical relevance of its collections. [10]

During initial conversations, UM's CLE administrator had remarked that most judges and lawyers are quite willing to participate on these panels, and my experience has confirmed this judgment. In Mississippi, CLE speakers are not permitted to accept payment for their services (a huge plus for budget-conscious repositories!). In return for their appearance on the panel, attorneys and judges garner a certain amount of prestige among their peers as well as CLE credit for their speaking role.

IMPLEMENTATION

Once the panel was set and accreditation obtained, I submitted details on the program for inclusion in the state CLE calendar of upcoming events, the state CLE newsletter, and also the state bar newsletter. These were easy and also absolutely crucial tools for promoting CLE events, as they are reviewed by attorneys across the state. Regardless, I did not neglect the more traditional public relations formats, such as institutional press releases and newsletters; campus flyers; and announcements on campus and local websites, calendars, and e-mail listservs. Finally, I worked closely with the donor's family to develop a list of contacts that received personal invitations from the archives. Every form of publicity included mention that one hour of CLE credit was available for those lawyers attending.

MPA mailed approximately 150 to 200 letters for each CLE program. Recipients included the immediate and extended family of the donor; a comprehensive list of former law clerks; neighbors, friends, and political allies; former colleagues on the bench; and all current members of that particular court. The archives also sent invitations to all officers of the state bar and board members of the Mississippi Bar Foundation. Although most recipients were not expected to attend, the time involved in printing the letters and addressing the envelopes was still worthwhile. After all, the invitations provided an opportunity to inform influential members of the bar and potential future donors about the Modern Political Archives and to impress them with the care and attention provided to its holdings.

With regards to MPA's first CLE program, the archives also sent letters to the donor families of its unprocessed legal collections, inviting them to attend the event and also explaining that their set of papers would be featured in an upcoming program sometime in the next few years. This step proved particularly constructive, as all recipients responded gratefully, and family members associated with two other judicial collections attended the Hawkins program and met the archivist.

Because earning CLE credit is a strong motivation for many of those attending, I made careful arrangements to follow reporting protocols. In Mississippi, sponsors are required to pay a $1.50 fee per credit hour for each Mississippi attorney seeking to obtain credit for attending the event. Fortunately, UM's CLE administrator volunteered to pay for the fees, and she also supplied the necessary forms for the lawyers to complete and turn in at the end of the program. MPA simply supplied an estimate on the number expected to attend and picked up the attendance forms the day before the event. The archives then prepared a registration table to greet visitors at the event. The table held a sign-in sheet requesting contact information for news on future MPA events as well as the CLE forms. Lawyers dropped off their completed CLE forms after the program at the registration table, and MPA delivered this paperwork to the CLE administrator the following day.

After the first program, I belatedly learned that judges and court-related personnel were also required to earn twelve hours of continuing judicial education (CJE). Thus, MPA sought accreditation from the Mississippi Judicial College for its second program on Judge J. P. Coleman. The standards for gaining accreditation approval were almost identical as those in the CLE policy. As the Mississippi Judicial College is located on the University of Mississippi campus, only a few phone calls proved necessary to obtain CJE approval. Consequently, at the Coleman event, the registration table held both the CJE and CLE forms.

To impress upon audience members the historic value of the collections, MPA installed two exhibit cases featuring material from the papers for each event. I also erected a temporary display for the event on a table at the front of the room where the program occurred. In addition, MPA offered each donor's family the opportunity to schedule a behind-the-scenes tour of its facility to discuss the details involved in processing archival collections, to view a selection of presidential letters and other significant documents from its holdings, and to inspect where their relation's collection resides within the stacks. These tours impress upon the donor's family the institutional resources committed to the preservation of the material and also indicate the value and respect that the university accords the collection.

RESULTS

The amount of time and energy dedicated to organizing both of these events proved well worth the effort. Several methods of assessment support this judgment. The first mode involves a simple head count. As mentioned previously, the department generally considers an audience of thirty or more a success. I began to suspect that the Hawkins program might exceed that number soon after publicity on the program began to appear. In the weeks leading up to the event, special collections received several dozen inquiries over the phone or via e-mail about the program. And although letters of invitation stated that no RSVP was necessary, several recipients communicated their intent to attend. Fortunately, these expectations provided sufficient warning for the archives to increase the number of CLE attendance forms, audience chairs, and handouts. For the first program honoring Chief Justice Armis Hawkins, seventy people attended. Despite statewide severe weather on the day of Judge J. P. Coleman's program in March 2011, the count rose to seventy-six.

Anecdotal evidence also indicates the value of the effort. Immediately following each event, numerous audience members sought me out to convey their pleasure in attending and their new interest in the archives. The family members of both donors also expressed their delight repeatedly. In fact, Judge Coleman's son wrote an appreciative letter to the chancellor: "My father would have been honored and pleased with the scholarly quality of this program. His wisdom in donating his judicial papers to the University of Mississippi, which he first visited in the fall of 1931 to bring a load of sweet potatoes to barter for his tuition, was validated by this program."[11] Obviously, a written testament such as this to the presiding administrator of one's institution is highly valued. The chancellor's chief of staff personally conveyed the news that several members of the state legislature had inquired about the programs, and the director of the law school library remarked that several individuals had commented to her favorably about the last program in the days that followed. By means of these positive communications, audience members and donors' families have thus become advocates to UM institutional leaders for MPA and its mission.

Finally, surveys provide another means of assessment. In fact, CLE-accredited events in Mississippi must offer attendees the opportunity to complete an evaluation questionnaire. UM's institutional review board (IRB) reviews and approves all human research conducted under the auspices of the institution.[12] This obligation extends to the most innocent of surveys. Fortunately, I had previously completed a three-hour online IRB course several years earlier to receive certification for conducting human research. For the judicial series, a renewal of certification required a much shorter online refresher course and the submission of an application form seeking IRB approval for each separate survey. It is important to be aware that IRB approval may or may not be necessary at different institutions for such relatively innocuous audience surveys, so consultation with that office is necessary. In fact, recent communication with UM's IRB indicated that certification for such instruments is no longer necessary, although they still require applications for approval. If certification is compulsory, you should factor in the time required to gain certification as well as for submitting applications for IRB approval.

In a 2010 survey on outreach activities conducted by special collections repositories, the Association of Research Libraries found that approximately a "third of all respondents have no formal means in place to evaluate events."[13] Those who do assess programming rely overwhelmingly on attendance and anecdotal feedback, with only a small number utilizing formal evaluations. Surveys, however, are useful tools. Most obviously, they provide quantifiable data for analyzing audience feedback. This information is particularly useful for institutional and accreditation reports. Surveys also offer a means for examining specifics related to the planning and execution of the program—issues like publicity, scheduling, and venue, as well as suggestions for topics and speakers in upcoming programs. Responses on these matters can confirm current arrangements or indicate the need for changing preparations in subsequent events.

MPA surveys for the CLE events were voluntary and anonymous. Of the seventy who attended the Hawkins program, seventeen completed and turned in an evaluation form—a response rate of approximately 24 percent. For the second program on Judge Coleman, seventeen of the seventy-six members of the audience completed the survey, about 22 percent. In both cases demographic information provided by respondents in the first question reinforced informal observations at the events themselves. Each crowd consisted primarily of lawyers, judges, community residents, and family and friends of the donor. A much smaller percentage of faculty and students attended each program. The second query asked if the respondent had ever before attended an exhibit or function at the archives and special collections, and the majority indicated that this was their first visit. Taken together, the responses to the first two questions indicate that MPA succeeded in attracting an audience from the targeted profession with little previous experience or awareness of the archives.

Those who completed the surveys cited a variety of methods by which they learned about the event (the focus of the third question), and no one format stands out as particularly significant. This result differs from the personal impressions I received through conversations and other communications indicating that the CLE announcements and the personal invitations were particularly effective.

Questions 4, 5, and 6 inquired about the quality of the programming: "Did this program advance your knowledge and understanding of the topic?" (Very much/Somewhat/Not much at all); "Overall, how would you rate this program?" (Excellent/Very good/Good/Acceptable/Poor); and "Would you attend more archives and special collections events or exhibits in the future or recommend them to others?" (Yes/No). Responses were overwhelmingly positive for all three questions, with only four individuals giving a lower rating of "Somewhat" and six responding with "Very good." All respondents indicated that they would return for future functions. The open-ended request for comments at the end of the survey contained the only negative remarks, and they focused on the unusual warmth in the room on one occasion, a request for more comfortable chairs, and the need for better directional marking within the library.

Question 7 briefly outlined the collections to be featured in future law-related programs and asked for suggestions on speakers and topics. Several of the recommendations from the survey will prove helpful as the archives plans these events.

I should note that neither of these CLE programs seemed to have any impact upon researcher use of the collections themselves. Those legal scholars who have consulted the papers appear to have learned about their existence through other means.[14] Although members of the Mississippi bar may not contribute much to the pool of patrons who utilize the collections for research, they do constitute a group with an inherent interest in preserving the history of their profession. Furthermore, through its participation in the CLE program, the archives supports the mission of the university in providing lifelong learning to professionals.[15] By offering an academic format to disseminate knowledge about the collection and the donor, MPA provides a venue for this particular constituency to earn the CLE credits required by the bar.[16]

The added virtue of this particular form of outreach is that it also permits the archives to educate a segment of the population on the value and historical relevance of the collections and the repository. Because lawyers tend to donate generous amounts of money to the university and typically occupy many of the seats of power in government, these "resource allocators" can serve as especially powerful outside advocates for the archives. Happily, in this particular case, outreach and advocacy go hand and hand.

LESSONS LEARNED

Several factors contributed to the success of these CLE programs. Among these were advance consultations with the university's CLE administrator and examination of the accrediting commission's requirements. Advertisement of the programs in the Mississippi State Bar's newsletter as well as the state's CLE calendar and newsletter proved essential in promoting the events. Also important were the personal invitations sent to the donor's family, friends, and associates, as well as leaders in the Mississippi State Bar and individuals at my own institution with a vested interest in the topic.

A panel of three to four speakers permitted the programs to address different aspects of the collection donor's career and also enabled me to include at least one scholar in order to enhance the academic nature of the events. Exhibiting collection material and offering behind-the-scenes tours to the donor's families highlighted the value of the records and the university's commitment to their preservation.

Finally, formally assessing each event with a survey allowed me to sample the demographics of the audience and provided feedback on publicity, the venue, and the success of each program. In addition, the survey elicited ideas for similar events in the future.

CONCLUSION

This case study has considered only two CLE programs that took place in July 2010 and March 2011. I anticipate planning at least one more event during spring 2014, with others taking place in the future as the archives brings more and more collections out of the backlog. The development of a long-running programming series is a great way to reconnect periodically with a targeted audience. The extended nature of the outreach will allow the archives to build a network of informed individuals and create a good impression of the repository in the legal community. Meanwhile, the *Mississippi Law Journal* has expressed eagerness to publish future addresses from the series, and one of their recent issues included a biographical account of Judge J. P. Coleman featuring facsimile reproductions of documents from the collection. [17]

The CLE programs may prove fruitful in other ways. Working with the library's development officer, I will explore the possibility of conducting a direct-mail campaign to raise funds specifically to support the preservation, processing, and promotion of its legal collections. Invitation lists and sign-in registrations from the events will provide the basis for developing contacts. The success of the CLE programs also provides a rationale for MPA to request financial support from the Mississippi Bar Foundation for processing expenses as well as the creation of a traveling exhibit on the importance of preserving judicial papers that could be used at local and state bar events. [18] Such a display would provide an additional venue for educating judges and attorneys about the historic value of the records while also promoting the archives and perhaps inspiring other judges to consider donating their files.

Continuing legal education may not be an option for repositories that possess little or no significant legal collections. Instead, archivists should ponder the possibilities offered by other professional continuing education programs as it relates to the holdings in their own institutions. Consider the focus of your collecting policy and the strengths of your holdings, and then talk to continuing education personnel on your campus or in your community. Do you have papers concerned with medical topics and health care? How about accounting records in the form of old financial and business ledgers? And almost any archive can work with educators to create a program on using primary resources for lesson plans in elementary and secondary schools. Continuing education programming is an opportunity for a repository to engage a targeted professional demographic on the subject of the archival mission as it relates to their own interests, and it is also a method for integrating the archive further into the teaching and community service functions of the parent institution. This aspect in turn reinforces the value of the repository to administrators and resource allocators.

Leigh McWhite *is the political papers archivist and associate professor at the University of Mississippi.*

NOTES

1. Two recent overviews on the subject are Jeffrey A. Cantor, *Lifelong Learning and the Academy: The Changing Nature of Continuing Education* (Hoboken, NJ: A. Wiley, 2006), and Arthur L. Wilson and Elisabeth R. Hayes, eds., *Handbook of Adult and Continuing Education* (San Francisco: Jossey-Bass, 2000).

2. I presented an earlier version of this essay at the 2011 meeting of the International Council on Archives' Section on University and Research Institution Archives (ICA/SUV) in Edmonton, Alberta, Canada.

3. Michael de L. Landon, *The University of Mississippi School of Law: A Sesquicentennial History* (Jackson: University Press of Mississippi, 2006).

4. For more information about the Modern Political Archives, see its home page: "Modern Political Archives: Introduction," *University of Mississippi Libraries: Archives and Special Collections*, accessed June 18, 2013, http://www.olemiss.edu/depts/general_library/archives/political.

5. The archival literature contains very little on the management of judicial papers. The most helpful source is Federal Judicial History Office, *A Guide to the Preservation of Federal Judges' Papers*, second edition (Washington, DC: Federal Judicial Center, 2009), accessed June 18, 2013, http://www.fjc.gov/public/pdf.nsf/lookup/judgpa2d.pdf/$File/judgpa2d.pdf . See also John N. Jacob, "The Lewis F. Powell Jr. Archives and the Contemporary Researcher," *Washington and Lee Law Review* 49, no. 1 (Winter 1992), 3–9.

6. "Finding Aid for the Armis Hawkins Collection," *University of Mississippi Libraries: Archives and Special Collections*, 2012, accessed January 19, 2014, http:// www.olemiss.edu/depts/general_library/archives/finding_aids/MUM01718.html .

7. The following is a useful resource for planning archival events, although the activities described herein predated its publication: Russell D. James and Peter J. Wosh, *Public Relations and Marketing for Archives* (Chicago: Society of American Archivists, 2011).

8. "Continuing Legal Education," *The University of Mississippi Division of Outreach and Continuing Education*, accessed June 18, 2013, http://www.outreach.olemiss.edu/

cle. I am grateful to Renee Moore, director of professional development at the University of Mississippi, for her assistance with this project and sharing her knowledge of CLE programs in general.

9. "State of Mississippi Rules and Regulations for Mandatory Continuing Legal Education," *State of Mississippi Judiciary*, August 1, 1994, accessed June 18, 2013, http://courts.ms.gov/rules/msrulesofcourt/continuing_legal_education.pdf .

10. "Finding Aid for the J. P. Coleman Collection," *University of Mississippi Libraries: Archives and Special Collections*, 2012, accessed January 19, 2014, http://www.olemiss.edu/depts/general_library/archives/finding_aids/MUM01734.html.

11. Copy of letter in my possession.

12. "Institutional Review Board," *The University of Mississippi*, accessed June 18, 2013, http://www.research.olemiss.edu/irb.

13. Association of Research Libraries, *SPEC Kit 317: Special Collections Engagement* (Washington, DC: Association of Research Libraries, 2010), p. 12. Front matter in this report is available for free online at "SPEC Kit 317: Special Collections Engagement," *Association of Research Libraries*, August 2010, accessed June 18, 2013, http://publications.arl.org/Special-Collections-Engagement-SPEC-Kit-317.

14. MPA made a concerted effort to promote the collection to researchers by posting online finding aids; adding collection MARC records to the library catalog; inserting collection descriptions and links into relevant departmental online subject guides; providing collection information to the Federal Judicial Center for their biographical database ("Biographical Director of Federal Judges, 1789–Present," *Federal Judicial Center*, accessed June 18, 2013, http://www.fjc.gov/history/home.nsf/page/judges.html); contacting the relevant court libraries/archives; and submitting announcements to the H-Law discussion list ("H-LAW," *American Society for Legal History*, accessed June 18, 2013, http://www.h-net.org/~law).

15. "Vision, Mission and Core Values," *University of Mississippi*, accessed February 12, 2014, http://www.olemiss.edu/aboutum/mission.html. Dorothy T. Frye explores one particular aspect of the connections between institutional missions and their archival repositories in "Linking Institutional Missions to University and College Archives Programs: The Land-Grant Model," *American Archivist* 56 (Winter 1993), 36–52.

16. Patricia J. Rettig argues effectively that "archives should maximize opportunities that already exist and integrate themselves into their constituents' lives. Presenting the archives as part of what a potential researcher or donor is already doing can prove the relevance of the archives to its constituents" ["An Integrative Approach to Archival Outreach: A Case Study of Becoming Part of the Constituents' Community," *Journal of Archival Organization* 5, no. 3 (2007), 31–46].

17. Leigh McWhite, "A Selection of Archival Documents: J. P. Coleman and the U.S. Court of Appeals for the Fifth Circuit," *Mississippi Law Journal* 82, no. 7 (2013), 1245–70. Items featured in the article were previously featured in the exhibit cases installed for the program.

18. The Mississippi Bar Foundation is a nonprofit entity concerned with "supplying essential information and ideas for the solution of current legal issues in the public interest and to improve the administration of justice." Its statement of purpose includes "sponsoring significant legal research, education and training projects." ("MS Bar Foundation History & Purpose," The Mississippi Bar, accessed 12 February 2014, http://msbar.org/programs-affiliates/ms-bar-foundationiolta/history-purpose.aspx).

FOUR

Staying Connected

Engaging Alumni and Students to Digitize the Carl "Pappy" Fehr Choral Music Collection

Amy C. Schindler, College of William & Mary

The Earl Gregg Swem Library's Special Collections Research Center at the College of William & Mary in Williamsburg, Virginia, faces an issue not uncommon in archives: a large volume of deteriorating and under-described scrapbooks. As a first but important step to address this problem, Swem's special collections has created a partnership with alumni and current students to begin rehousing, digitizing, and describing the dozens of scrapbooks about the William & Mary Choir and Chorus. A project aimed at bringing alumni and friends to Swem Library to tackle the preservation and access needs of scrapbooks, led by two alumni of the university's choral music program, was launched in early 2011. Not unusually, the alumni had maintained close relationships with fellow choir members and other friends from their college days. The alumni are also part of the William & Mary class of 1975's "Staying Connected: Together Serving Others" initiative to volunteer with other alumni and current students on community service projects through which they will reconnect and maintain connections with the university. As "Staying Connected" was launching, the alumni remembered the collection of their beloved choral music director that they viewed in Swem Library's special collections. By building on an existing network of alumni, we have been able to address issues of access and preservation facing the scrapbooks that we had brought to the attention of the alumni.

Few of these volunteers had previously visited Swem Library's special collections before or even had an idea that the department existed or what it does. While we embarked on the project to bring volunteers into the special collections with goals of digitizing and preserving material related to the university's choral music program, we also saw an opportunity to expand our audience. The alumni and students who were part of the choral music program should naturally be major users of this material, but we also hoped to interest them in other parts of the library and special collections having nothing to do with their choir experiences. We expected they could help us build the department's holdings related to their years at the university or other areas, such as rare books. While some student researchers graduate with an appreciation for the resources they were able to access in Swem Library's special collections for papers and other projects, this initiative provided us with an opportunity to create a connection for alumni and students with special collections outside of course work. This connection would not have a due date at the end of a semester or the submission of a thesis to earn their degrees.

PLANNING

In 2009, Swem Library's special collections began planning for how best to handle the complicated and increasing preservation needs of the scrapbooks among its holdings. Preliminary staff research into the needs of scrapbooks included reading about the efforts of the University of Illinois to care for their scrapbook collection.[1] Staff member Steven Bookman was tasked with further investigation and writing a report to guide the future actions of special collections staff appropriate to the resources available in Swem Library. The report provided a summary of the peculiar needs of scrapbooks, further resources for staff, and a plan of concrete steps to address the needs of Swem's collections.[2] Among the scrapbooks identified as candidates for further preservation were those about the choral music program due to their varying conservation needs as well as the large time range over which they were created. As of 2009, most scrapbooks in Swem Library's special collections have been placed in archival boxes upon processing, but there were also those that were stored on shelves without benefit of an archival box. Very few of the scrapbooks that were in archival boxes had additional padding or were interleaved. Many of the boxes were too large, too small, overly full, or oriented upright when they should be stored flat.

A key component of the department's plan was to begin a preservation survey of its scrapbook holdings, which was begun by two volunteers the same year the report was drafted. Over the previous two summers, the department had completed a preservation survey of its university archives and manuscript collection holdings with the help of graduate student fellows. The data gathered in the earlier survey was now used to identify the collections that included one or more scrapbooks. One volunteer assigned to the scrapbook project was an undergraduate student considering a career in the library, archives, or museums field, while the other volunteer was a recent graduate from another university considering a graduate degree to pursue a career in archives. While one of the volunteers pursued an item-level survey of scrapbooks, the other began digitizing scrapbooks using either a flatbed scanner or camera, depending on the condition of the scrapbooks. The department also used student assistants to begin interleaving newly acquired scrapbooks when that treatment was identified as appropriate by the accessioning archivist. It became clear early on that the preservation of scrapbooks would largely have to be undertaken by a mix of volunteers and undergraduate students to be feasible at all.

In 2007 I met three alumni, Carol Plambeck and Ann and Mark Woolley, who had been passionate and enthusiastic members of the choral music program in the 1970s and continued to treasure that association. Traveling to Williamsburg from their homes in different states, they arranged to visit Swem Library's special collections in order to view the collection of their fondly remembered director of choral music, Dr. Carl "Pappy" Fehr. The Fehr papers are more than sixty cubic feet in size and include correspondence, concert programs, sheet music, hundreds of photographs, twenty-seven scrapbooks, dozens of concert recordings, and artifacts dating from the 1940s until Fehr's retirement in the 1970s, as well as material about student reunions from the 1970s and 1980s.[3]

Our alumni visitors spent several hours reminiscing over memorabilia and programs and were especially interested in the scrapbooks, which they had played a role in creating as students in the 1970s and which were deteriorating with the passage of years, losing carefully glued-in pieces with each turn of a page. The oldest scrapbooks in the Fehr collection date from the mid-1940s, and as those from the 1950s, they are in reasonably sound condition. During the 1950s it became customary for members of the both the choir and women's chorus to produce one joint scrapbook each academic year. Eventually, separate scrapbooks were produced by the choir and women's chorus, and by the 1970s it was not uncommon for more than one scrapbook to be produced by each group annually due to their growing size. The scrapbooks produced in the late 1960s and 1970s became more and more complex and include a variety of material types. The glue used in the 1970s especially has failed, and individual pieces, like personalized construction paper details and photos, fell out of place with each use of the volumes.

During this cordial visit with our alumni guests, I presented our options for better preserving and providing access to the scrapbooks. We discussed the time and resources required for the highest level of conservation, such as trained staff for the detailed conservation work or funds for a conservator to reconstruct the volumes, encapsulate pages, etc. We also discussed other options, including digitizing the scrapbooks, so that they could be available online to alumni everywhere, thereby reducing demand on the originals. This could then be followed by rehousing the scrapbooks, appropriate interleaving and disbinding, and padding within the boxes. Our first meeting was a great opportunity to reintroduce the Fehr papers to some of the alumni who are not only documented in the collection but also helped to create parts of it. Furthermore, these alumni had the chance to acquaint themselves with special collections and library staff. Before leaving, the alumni indicated they had additional material to donate to the collection. A formal proposal for financial support to digitize and care for the collection was not presented to the alumni, but I did convey the need for additional financial resources before any next steps could be explored. We stayed in touch, and during their next campus visit a few months later, the alumni donated material from their choir days to special collections. Due to their distance from campus, we did not expect these alumni to be able to become volunteers in the department but hoped we could count on them as supporters. Over the next two years, we stayed in irregular but friendly contact.

The William & Mary class of 1975's five-year initiative for their fortieth reunion, "Staying Connected: Together Serving Others," was the brainchild of alumnus Van Black. The goals of "Staying Connected" include creating and nurturing opportunities to bring alumni, current students, and university staff and organizations together in social and service settings.

In the early days of the "Staying Connected" initiative, alumni Ann and Mark Woolley contacted me to discuss an idea for a service project in Swem Library's special collections. They proposed a volunteer effort to digitize, rehouse, and further describe the choral music collection of Dr. Fehr. The volunteer project would address the preservation and access issues of Dr. Fehr's collection I had articulated and they had seen for themselves when they had visited it in special collections four years earlier. A conference call was quickly arranged between the Woolleys, special collections staff, and the library's director of development. During the conversation, the alumni explained the "Staying Connected" initiative and we discussed ideas for how to accomplish the digitization effort, including the need for additional supplies, equipment, and other resources that would be required. We also discussed how best to accommodate volunteers schedule wise: on a monthly basis or a couple times each year (monthly seemed like asking too much of everyone involved); what size groups to host (preferably ten to twenty); whether individuals could volunteer outside of the organized "Staying Connected" Saturdays (of course!); and the types of tasks best suited to volunteers (it depends on the individual). Financial support of the ongoing efforts was a part of the conversation from this first discussion, and while the library never made it a requirement, it was also clear that contribution of additional resources would be highly desirable to support the project.

As part of our planning for the volunteer day, I discussed with the Woolleys, mostly by e-mail, the maximum number of participants we could accommodate in Swem's special collections; registration; initial and ongoing communication with volunteers; orientation and training; the types of tasks it would be reasonable to ask volunteers to learn and undertake in a single day; the day's schedule; the number of library staff needed to train, supervise, and in some cases entertain volunteers; refreshments; and other details large and small. We were incredibly fortunate on multiple fronts: Our alumni friends are highly organized individuals and happy to take on many of the organizational details, including putting out a call for help through their network, printing name badges, and securing refreshments.

Swem Library staff members welcomed the alumni and were willing to cooperate on this new initiative with volunteers on a scale not previously undertaken in special collections. With the recent report and survey begun of the scrapbooks in special collections, we had an increased awareness of the particular needs of this format as well as the benefits of increased use and reduced wear and tear on the originals that digitization offered. It also worked to our advantage that, just before the first volunteer day, the library had hired a new fine arts librarian who was interested in the project as well as a special collections staff member responsible for the exhibits program and artifact care who also has excellent skills in graphic design and photography, which would be crucial in training and assisting volunteer digitizers.

IMPLEMENTATION

In advance of the first "Staying Connected" Saturday, staff prepared descriptions of several different tasks at a range of skill levels that volunteers could choose from, including: low-tech activities like rehousing scrapbooks and rehousing photographs; creating set lists of minimally identified recordings of concerts; scanning and describing photographs; and photographing and making scrapbooks available online. The task descriptions also included notes about the equipment involved and helpful skills, such as the ability to use a computer, camera, or specific software. These descriptions along with a schedule for the day were discussed and revised with the Woolleys, our alumni organizers, and then distributed to the registrants in advance as part of a welcome message from me on behalf of the library. While a secondary component of the project, the digitization and additional description of the hundreds of photographs, slides, and negatives in the Fehr collection is also being undertaken by volunteers. "Staying Connected" volunteers were able to complete the rehousing of the hundreds of photographs in the collection within the first year of the project. These individual images are not yet available online, but this remains a priority for the library in the near future.

Staff also prepared detailed instructions for each task to have on hand for staff and volunteers during the event. While of course special collections staff knew how to use the flatbed scanners, a camera, or other pieces of equipment, we wanted to have written instructions for each task so that volunteers and staff members from other library departments would have something to refer to if needed. Multiple tasks were assigned to each staff member to ensure we could rotate between jobs, especially if the popular ones, like photographing scrapbooks, would draw more volunteers than the more monotonous stations, like scanning photographs.

In preparation for the scanning event, we also needed to decide where the images of the scrapbooks would be hosted. Although the library had explored several other options in earlier scanning efforts, we made the decision to use Omeka as the online home for the scrapbooks, in large part because the library was already using the application for another purpose. We had experience with Omeka and the Scripto plugin that allows users to both transcribe and describe items. [4] The decisive factor in our decision to use Omeka was its capacity for online display and the fact that the Scripto plugin provided an easy avenue for volunteers to transcribe and describe each page of the scrapbooks online. [5]

While Swem Library has raised the possibility of buying new equipment with the alumni during our initial project discussion, to date existing library cameras and scanners have been sufficient. One volunteer does routinely bring his camera with him, but it has remained a tool for documenting the activities of the alumni, students, and friends. For the digitization project itself, the volunteers have used the department's scanner and two cameras already in use in special collections in addition to other cameras borrowed from the library's media center. Special collections also has two flatbed scanners in a staff area of the department. For "Staying Connected" Saturdays, one of these machines is moved to the reading room, where all volunteer activities take place. We are also able to borrow laptops for volunteers and staff to use from the library's pool of laptops available for checkout.

For our first "Staying Connected" Saturday, eight library staff members were present for all or part of the day. As the number of trained and returning volunteers stabilized, the number of staff present for the volunteers has decreased, and after three years it is more common for four staff members to be present.

A typical "Staying Connected" Saturday begins with a light breakfast in the library lobby, providing a chance for new and returning staff and volunteers to meet or become reacquainted. For the first three "Staying Connected" Saturdays, when many of the volunteers were alumni and new to the project and special collections, we took time to introduce the volunteers to the work that is done in our department and why it is so important that we acquire, preserve, and make available collections. This ninety-minute orientation included a general overview of handling materials, the finding aids, and outreach efforts, before the volunteers would begin their work with the collection.[6] While the first orientation session was about ninety minutes in length, we have shortened it as the groups of new volunteers for successive "Staying Connected" Saturdays have decreased. At the most recent event, new volunteers did not participate in a separate presentation but were instead given a basic care and handling overview by a staff member after the welcome and overview of the project at the beginning of the day.

The orientation is followed by a tour of Swem Library's special collections, including the storage areas, staff work areas, and public spaces, to reiterate points about outreach, access, digitization, and preservation that were addressed during the orientation. Finally, before lunch, the newcomers are introduced to the different tasks that the returning volunteers are working on that day and can begin to try their hand at one of them before lunch, which the group has together in the library.

After lunch, volunteers continue working on their chosen tasks for the day. Because the "Staying Connected" initiative wants to connect alumni with not just their alma mater but also current students, the Woolleys and the library's arts librarian have reached out to current members of the choral music program to participate in the volunteer days. Special collections also has a number of alumni donors and student assistants who were involved with music in one form or another as students, and we have made an effort to invite alumni and students from our own network to volunteer. While not all volunteers were or are members of the choir, there is usually a large number of past and current members of the choral music program, and inevitably at some point during the day, people will break into song in small groups, and often the entire group will join in. The singers are also understanding about those of us who do not sing. As one of the most loyal volunteers explains, someone has to sit in the chairs and be the audience!

As the nontechnical tasks, such as sleeving photographs and rehousing scrapbooks, have been completed, we have taken different approaches to ensure we are providing a variety of tasks that would interest people of different skill levels. After all of the photographs from Dr. Fehr's collection were rehoused in sleeves, we brought nonchoral music photographs out for our volunteers to work with from the University Archives Photograph Collection. Some of the volunteers enjoyed seeing these other parts of the collection, but there was also a desire to keep the project focused on the choral music aspect of student life. Because we want volunteers who are describing the already digitized scrapbooks and photographs to do so online instead of on paper, if they are not comfortable using one of the laptops made available, we will also pair students and older alumni and friends to work together. This allows the alumni who can identify people in the photographs by name to essentially work with a transcriber (see figure 4.1).

RESULTS

In its third year, the "Staying Connected" choral music project has held seven volunteer events in the library. The number of alumni, students, and friends attending has ranged from eleven to twenty-eight, with a typical group numbering fifteen to twenty people. The project has been well received by staff and library administration. Staff members have an opportunity to meet and work with people who often care passionately about the material they are handling because of their personal connection to it. Library administration appreciates that we are engaging alumni beyond visiting the library by having them actively participate in a service project in special collections that is ongoing. While in the library for the day, including breakfast, digitizing, lunch, more digitizing and de-

Figure 4.1. Alumni from the classes of 1955 and 1976 work with a current William & Mary student to identify members of the William & Mary Choir from a photograph during a February 2013 volunteer day in Swem Library's Special Collections

scribing, and visiting with each other in other parts of the library, the alumni volunteers have a chance to see (as well as hear from staff members) how students use and value the library as space as well as the resources available.

To date, most of the users of the collection have been the project alumni, volunteers, and friends and family with whom they share the scrapbooks, now online at http://scrcdigital.swem.wm.edu/collections/show/4. And they are naturally thrilled to see themselves, their former choir mates, and their director through the online scrapbooks they helped create.

Of course, the most obvious aspect of the project's success is that dozens of scrapbooks and hundreds of photographs are being digitized, described in more detail, and rehoused. To date, twenty-four of the collections' scrapbooks have been digitized and are available online. This is of course a great outcome, and we continue to see more and more descriptions being added remotely by alumni volunteers in between the "Staying Connected" Saturdays, which is a sure sign that the project—and Swem Library—is keeping the attention of its volunteers.

At the end of the first two "Staying Connected" Saturdays, we set aside time for the group of volunteers to sit down together to talk about what they got out of the day and offer suggestions for future project days. After each Saturday event, we also send an e-mail follow-up thanking people for their contributions and to share an update on our progress to date as well. This is also a group that is not afraid of photographs, and each "Staying Connected" Saturday a group photo is taken along with casual snapshots of people working together to digitize, rehouse, and describe material in special collections. Some of these photos are also shared. In addition, we have produced brief wrap-up news articles that are distributed to "Staying Connected's" group, which is part of the alumni association's online community (and not available to the public), via e-mail as well as publicized through the library's website and social media.

Through this project we have considerably strengthened a loose connection with alumni Ann and Mark Woolley, with whom I shared "Pappy" Fehr's scrapbooks for the first time in more than thirty years. The "Staying Connected" project continues to bring more alumni, students, and their friends and families into the library and into special collections, many of whom had not previously visited or probably did not even know that the department existed. While some of these visits have been one time only, most of the more than fifty volunteers to date have attended two or more "Staying Connected" Saturdays. Nearly every Saturday includes new volunteers. Some of them have even become users of special collections, some have become donors, and some have brought us more like-minded volunteers. The "Staying Connected" project has also helped alumni to reconnect with classmates and to make new friends among current students and with alumni from different classes.

The project has likewise introduced special collections to current students who had no previous contact with our department. Allowing students to see that the library is involved in a volunteer project on a campus where service projects are such an important part of student life is also a positive move for the library. One of the choir student volunteers brought another student organization he is affiliated with to special collections for a tour so they could see "their" archives in advance of the group's twenty-fifth anniversary. The group was excited that special collections then provided reproductions of items from their archives for the anniversary celebration as well as extra yearbooks that they shared with their alumni.

The project has led alumni and student volunteers to donate additional material related to the choral music program and other aspects of the university's history, as well as items for the rare book collection. For example, we have received a choir quilt, posters, programs, photographs, recordings, and other materials. Current students who have heard about the "Staying Connected" project have begun to deliver scrapbooks from the post–"Pappy" Fehr choir period to the archives, thus filling a gap in the choir history coverage. These students are also donating material related to other aspects of their William & Mary experience to the archives. We also continue to receive monetary donations from alumni, which enabled us to buy necessary supplies for rehousing and more recently allowed us to pay the wages of one student employee who has taken on responsibility for digitizing photographs and uploading the scrapbooks to Omeka between the Saturday sessions.

LESSONS LEARNED

The most important thing for a volunteer-driven digitization project to be successful is having a dedicated volunteer group as the base. This has been crucially important for us. We knew it would be desirable to digitize the scrapbooks and other material. Without committed alumni like Ann and Mark Woolley, who remembered a conversation with an archivist and cared enough to work with Swem Library to create this volunteer project and then involve their friends, other alumni, and students, this project would not have been attempted at this scale and continued to grow and evolve.

A practical measure to make new volunteers feel welcomed and to recognize veteran volunteers for their dedication and service is to provide nametags for each volunteer and whenever possible include a photo of the alum from the yearbook. Stickers have also been added to nametags to show the number of Saturdays a volunteer has attended.

To welcome the group to the library, a staff member designed a poster using a historical photograph of choir director Carl Fehr. The poster displayed both on the library's digital signs and a traditional paper copy is placed at the entrance to special collections for the day. This gesture, though small, has been noticed and remarked on by volunteers at each "Staying Connected" event.

We also make certain we have a small gift for the volunteers to show our thanks. At the first "Staying Connected" Saturday, special collections made copies of one of the choir's concerts on CDs for each participant.[7] The library has provided Swem logo–branded items, like notebooks, pencils, notecards, and flash drives. After a conversation with one of the veteran volunteers, we even ordered Swem Library–logo temporary tattoos for the following volunteer day during Homecoming weekend. The tattoos were a big hit with the volunteers and others who visited the library during Homecoming. We made certain to mail some to the volunteer who spawned the idea but was unable to join us on that particular Saturday.

After a few scrapbooks had been digitized and were uploaded to Omeka, a bookmark promoting the scrapbook website was designed. It is also meant to stimulate interest in the entire collection of "Pappy" Fehr and encourages people to contact special collections to learn more about the collection, the digitization project, and available concert recordings. The bookmark uses a choir concert poster from the 1970s as the basis for its design. The poster was actually donated by an alumnus after he began attending the "Staying Connected" Saturdays. These items are small tokens of our appreciation, but they also remind our alumni, students, and other volunteers of their time in Swem Library. Recently when I visited an alumna in her home to discuss a potential donation of books to the library, she was keen to point out that she was using one of the pencils from Swem Library's special collections to complete her daily word puzzle. This is the sort of affinity for and connection to the library and special collections we hoped the project would create.

It is also important to keep in mind that different constituents may have different objectives but that it is possible to find ways to work toward reaching everyone's goal. Our alumni wanted to help people reconnect with classmates and the university while preserving a slice of William & Mary history centered on "Pappy" Fehr's years at the college. Our library staff shared these goals, but we also wanted to engage the alumni, students, and other volunteers with Swem Library, special collections, and our branch library in the music department.

As special collections does not yet have an online database for its image collection, descriptions are being captured off line in a legacy database. After the first four volunteer days resulted in lower-than-expected scanning and description results, we made the decision to move from a Microsoft Access database to an Excel spreadsheet for more rapid data entry. This resulted in fewer frustrations for the volunteers and heightened productivity. Recently, we have also hired an undergraduate student for the monotonous task of scanning the photographs, slides, and negatives in the collection outside of the volunteer days to allow volunteers to focus on the description tasks during their limited time with the material in the library.

During the first "Staying Connected" event, volunteers were working on different floors due to space and equipment considerations within special collections. But we realized quickly that this stretched our staff resources and isolated some of our volunteers. Since then, we have kept all volunteers in the reading room. After all, in many cases they were there to see each other just as much as they were to assist with the digitization project.

In retrospect, in our effort to offer tasks that appealed to a wide range of skills and interests during those early sessions, we were trying to do too much and spread our staff too thin. We also learned that we needed to allow more time for staff to prepare for each work session and to tie up loose ends afterward.

I had hoped that over time the library could decrease the number of staff as repeat volunteers have become familiar with the tasks and need less guidance. However, even after six volunteer sessions, we still find it helpful, if not essential, especially for the morning session, to have several staff members present as veteran volunteers reacquaint themselves with equipment and software and new volunteers need to be trained.

If Swem Library or special collections had begun this project on its own without identifying committed alumni partners like the Woolleys who could drum up support for it within their own network, I am doubtful that we could have found volunteers as numerous and as loyal. The Woolleys reached out early on to the current director of choral music to let him know about the project as well as to invite current students to "Staying Connected" Saturdays. The library's fine arts and music librarian also used her network and contacts with students in her branch library to connect current students with the initiative. Special collections has invited more recent alumni who worked in special collections or are donors who were involved in choral music to "Staying Connected" Saturdays. While some have attended, none have (yet) turned into regular volunteers. While our committed alumni volunteers began the project equipped with their Christmas card list and the then-fledgling "Staying Connected" program's listserv, now their recruitment efforts are reaching current students and alumni who graduated as far back as the 1950s.

CONCLUSION

The focus of the "Staying Connected" volunteer project remains digitizing, rehousing, and describing material in Swem Library's special collections related to choral music at William & Mary. As the scrapbooks from Dr. Fehr's era (1940s–1970s) are completed, efforts will move forward in time to digitize the more recent donations. The oldest a cappella group on campus has also donated a collection of scrapbooks and other material from its early history as a result of the "Staying Connected" volunteers' efforts. The expectation is—and rightly so—that eventually these scrapbooks will be digitized and available online for all to enjoy. Staff are in contact with a variety of student organizations, and once all choral music scrapbooks have been digitized, volunteer efforts will shift to the wind symphony orchestra, service organizations, fraternities and sororities, and other campus groups. Special collections would certainly like to begin the digitization of nonchoral music materials, but we are in need of interested volunteers or donors willing to fund student assistants to do the digitization.

Finally, through off-campus demonstrations by alumni volunteers, mentions in the alumni magazine's class notes section, and word of mouth, we hope that more alumni volunteers will participate, even if it is remotely by describing individual scrapbook pages online. Some of our regular volunteers have discussed hosting a day for an alumni get-together in another city, so they can share their work and train others on how anyone can add to the description of material online. We are confident volunteers will continue to return to Swem Library to digitize and are very pleased that our alumni volunteers are excited enough to organize gatherings in other cities.

Since our earliest discussions about digitizing the scrapbooks of Dr. Fehr and the positive experience with the resulting "Staying Connected" project, staff and the alumni who proposed the idea all wished to broaden the scope to bring in cheerleaders, athletes, fraternities, sororities, and all other alumni, whatever their interests as students. Our hope is to not only rekindle the connections to alumni who have been out of touch with the university but also to strengthen the link between current students and those alumni who already feel a bond to William & Mary. The library can accomplish this, establishing meaningful, participatory relationships as described in this chapter. It would be a true measure of success if we could retain many of the current choir volunteers as the project's focus shifts to materials from other eras and organizations. While staying connected to the university as alumni drove the creation of this project, the process of making connections with alumni as well as students has been a transformative one for special collections and has provided a model for connecting with volunteers and donors going forward.

Amy C. Schindler *is the director of archives and special collections at the University of Nebraska Omaha. Until December 2013 she was university archivist at the College of William & Mary.*

NOTES

The author would like to acknowledge and thank Swem Library colleague Ute Schechter for her editorial assistance and advice in the writing of this chapter.

1. Jennifer Hain Teper, "An Introduction to Preservation Challenges and Potential Solutions for Scrapbooks in Archival Collections," *Journal of Archival Organization* 5, no. 3 (2007), accessed May 1, 2013, https://connections.ideals.illinois.edu/works/26024; Jennifer Hain Teper and Emily F. Shaw, "Planning for Conservation of Archival Scrapbook Collections," *Archival Products News* 14, no. 4 (2007), accessed May 1, 2013, http://www.archival.com/newsletters/apnewsvol14no4.pdf.

2. "Appraisal and Processing Committee Scrapbook Processing Report," 2009, available in the department's files.

3. The finding aid for the Carl A. "Pappy" Fehr papers is available online at http://scdb.swem.wm.edu/index.php?p=collections/controlcard&id=6590.

4. Swem Library implemented a locally hosted instance of Omeka in early 2011 as the home for Swem's Civil War digitization and crowdsourced transcription project. The online transcription of special collections' complete unpublished holdings from the Civil War era is one part of Swem Library's "From Fights to Rights: The Long Road to a More Perfect Union" project to commemorate the 150th anniversary of the Civil War and the 50th anniversary of the Civil Rights Movement. "From Fights to Rights: The Long Road to a More Perfect Union," *Swem Library*, accessed May 2, 2013, https://swem.wm.edu/news/fights-rights; "Scripto Instructions," *Swem Library's Special Collections Research Center Staff Wiki*, accessed 2 May 2013, http://scrc.wmwikis.net/Scripto+Instructions.

5. Omeka is a project of the Roy Rosenzweig Center for History and New Media, George Mason University, and is billed as a "free, flexible, and open source web-publishing platform for the display of library, museum, archives, and scholarly collections and exhibitions." Further, Omeka bills itself as "designed with non-IT specialists in mind, allowing users to focus on content and interpretation rather than programming. It brings Web 2.0 technologies and approaches to academic and cultural websites to foster user interaction and participation. It makes top-shelf design easy with a simple and flexible templating system." "Omeka: Serious Web Publishing," accessed May 2, 2013, http://omeka.org/about.

6. The presentation we used was based on a longer training session offered by Drexel University Archives, which itself was adapted from the CLIR PACSCL Processing Boot Camp with permission. Thank you to Rebecca Goldman of LaSalle University, formerly of Drexel, for her advice on training a large group of volunteers and for sharing Drexel's slides.

7. Recordings of the concerts on reel-to-reel tapes as well as commercially produced LPs were previously digitized with the support of funds raised by choir and chorus alumni who sang under Dr. Fehr and are available for a nominal fee.

FIVE

"Pin"pointing Success

Assessing the Value of Pinterest and Historypin for Special Collections Outreach

Mark Baggett, Rabia Gibbs, and Alesha Shumar,
University of Tennessee

According to new media theorist Lev Manovich, to understand modern users' needs, it is important to recognize that many information-age activities regularly blur the line between work and social interaction, with users using the same interface for very different purposes.[1] For example, we are seeing more and more researchers accessing information not just through databases and traditional websites but also increasingly through social media. This chapter outlines the University of Tennessee (UT) Libraries' effort to improve access and discovery of its unique digitized content by using two social media platforms—Historypin and Pinterest—to market our digital resources and create outreach opportunities to reach new users outside of our academic library's traditional audience.

Initiated in summer 2012 as a collaboration between special collections and digital initiatives, the primary goal of the project was to determine if hosting collections on social media sites increased the discovery and usage of digitized special collections materials. In addition to exploring new ways for users to discover and engage with digital content, we also wanted to assess our return on investment and the long-term feasibility of using Web 2.0 tools to support the library's outreach goals while utilizing limited staff time and budget. Our project findings revealed that using Historypin and Pinterest exposed our digital collections to a wider population and enhanced the sociability and shareability of our posted content. In addition, we learned that despite the similarities in concept, Historypin and Pinterest have platform-specific functionalities that require different procedures for ingesting content and individualized outreach strategies to make the most of platform features and built-in audiences.

PLANNING

Our project originated out of an informal discussion about ways to enhance the visibility of and interaction with UT Libraries' special collections materials. Some suggestions included using augmented reality to increase user engagement with digitized photographs or incorporating data visualization to enhance the scholarly use of our research materials, such as our digitized Civil War diaries. While exciting, these ideas required a significant amount of administrative buy-in, financial investment for software platforms, and personnel time to ingest and maintain content. As a result we tried to look for smaller, more manageable tools that addressed our project queries in a meaningful way but were also sustainable for long-term analysis. Other selection parameters included:

- no subscription cost
- established user base
- user-friendly interfaces for both end users and content managers
- clear but adequately descriptive metadata elements to identify items
- ability to create added value for hosted content
- ability to gather usage data (analytics)
- ability to link the content back to the university's digital collections webpage
- ability to target a demographic outside of the traditional academic library audience

In addition, we wanted the platforms to address findability, sociability, and shareability. *Findability* refers to sharing digital content on platforms in addition to the library website in order to make them easier to find. *Sociability* is defined as allowing users to comment on images and make personal connections with the library. Finally, *shareability* refers to creating mechanisms for users to share digitized materials with other users, further improving access and discovery.

The library initially selected Pinterest because of its popularity. Pinterest is a free, fully hosted third-party content-sharing platform that allows users to upload and share image-based media, such as photographs and video, on separate themed "boards." With a heavy focus on images, content can be uploaded, "repinned" from other users' boards, or sourced directly from the Internet. Users can comment on and like "pinned" items, share them by repinning them on their own boards, and follow other boards based on personal interest. In addition, users can create community boards and invite others to pin content. For our project, we tried to take advantage of all of these social aspects.

In the end the main factor for selecting Pinterest was its well-established user base. Pinterest is the fourth most popular social networking site, with more than 85,500,000 unique monthly visitors.[2] This is likely due to Pinterest's ease of use for both finding and pinning new content related to users' diverse interests. However, it is important to note that the demographics are heavily skewed, with 82 percent of users being female and an overrepresentation in the southeast region, a factor that would later affect the selection process for the project.[3]

Overall, Pinterest addressed all of our criteria except for allowing us to create added value for digital content. By *added value* we mean we wanted to expand beyond just displaying content as we do on our traditional website and add context to hosted material to make it more meaningful to the end user. While the project originally specified only exploring one social media platform, we decided to try to find a second platform that was conceptually similar to Pinterest but had a feature that allowed us to add value to a digital collection.

While the initial idea of using augmented reality seemed promising, we agreed that we needed to find a more cost-effective, time-efficient, and user-friendly method to engage with people. This led us to explore the idea of mashups. Mashups use content from more than one source to create new and unique ways to experience that content. While there are many different types of mashups, the most popular are map based, taking data from one or more sources and displaying it on a map in a single interface.[4]

After reviewing several software options, including Viewshare, a free application developed by the Library of Congress, we selected Historypin as our second platform for several reasons, including its ease of implementation and the ability to add value to digital content using the platform's geolocation-based "pinning" tool.[5] Created by We Are What We Do, Historypin is a free, community-based, third-party website on which users can share and comment on historical materials—including images, video, and audio—in album, display, exhibit, or tour formats. Historypin collections can be browsed by keywords, dates, locations, and institutions and include original links for the user to navigate back to full digital collections on the contributors' websites.

The main reason for choosing Historypin was the platform's ability to "pin" images to geographic locations on Google Maps, allowing content managers to create mashups of historical images with contemporary views by overlaying photographs on top of Google Street View images. The effect is best achieved through Historypin's fading tool, which allows users to fade the overlaying image into the street view underneath for a real-time comparison of the past and present. In addition, the platform also provides content contributors with the ability to create tours of their digital content. Tours can add value by creating a chronological or narrative context for digital materials, augmenting the way that users experience and understand content.[6]

Historypin and Pinterest combined met our eight predetermined selection criteria for the project. Both products were free, with user- and content manger–friendly interfaces, basic metadata elements, the ability to link back to original collections hosted by UT Libraries, and user demographics outside of the library's traditional user community. Pinterest had a broader and more established user base, but Historypin allowed us to add value to the materials through mashups and tours. Most importantly, both platforms had built-in analytic tools to compare data against the Google Analytics from our library site.

IMPLEMENTATION

With our platforms selected, we needed to decide what digital content to use for the project. Our selection criteria included a review of UT Libraries' current digital collections for materials that 1) had been hosted on the library's main digital collections webpage for at least a year, 2) had documented usage based on user requests for the physical and digitized material, and 3) included strikingly visual content. We wanted to use materials hosted on the library's website because the content had already been vetted for copyright and because of our built-in Google Analytics. Materials heavily used in both a physical and digital format were selected not only because they were the most frequently requested material but also because we needed established usage statistics for comparative analysis.

Though we had chosen Pinterest first, we started the project with Historypin because we were already aware that the ingestion process was more time intensive based on an initial comparison.[7] The following digitized materials, originally hosted on the library website, were selected for initial ingestion into Historypin: two collections of images with a strong connection to Tennessee (Photographs of Tennessee Cities, MS.0951, and the University of Tennessee Photograph and Slide Collection, AR.0018) and two collections of broader national or historical interest (the Clarence Brown Papers, MS.0702, and the W. C. Robinson Collection Scopes Trial Photographs, MS.1091). Clarence Brown was a prominent UT alumnus who became a well-known Hollywood director and producer, and many of the images document Hollywood of the 1930s and 1940s. The collection of Scopes trial photographs documents scenes in the courtroom and the local community, as well as portraits of many of the participants involved in the trial. Because of their large scale, we only used a small subset from the original collections. Scaling down was not only important for manageability, but it also helped us mimic the "typical" collections in the Historypin platform, which were much smaller and condensed in terms of theme or topic. This was the same selection criteria we used for Pinterest.

The time to upload and describe a digital collection was one of the factors we measured closely in each platform to determine return on investment and long-term sustainability. In terms of implementation, Historypin used significantly less resources than required to host a digital collection on our own library website, particularly staff time. Compared to Pinterest, however, Historypin was comparatively more time intensive due to the level of metadata description and increased functionality, such as arranging content in a desired order and pinning it to a geographic location.

A total of 30 hours was required to upload 128 images to Historypin, averaging out to approximately 14 minutes per pinned item. Based on the average salary of $18 per hour (averaging faculty, staff, and student library assistant salaries), the total cost was $540, or nearly $4.25 per pinned item. It is important to note that scanning the special collections material is not included in this estimation; all content selected for the primary phase of the project was already digitally available. Two of the main challenges were mapping the metadata to display correctly and utilizing the geolocation features.

For our library's digital collections metadata, the library repurposes descriptive metadata from special collections' online finding aids. In addition to primary fields, such as title and dates, these records also include such information as creator, copyright, and Library of Congress subject headings. Although the exact number of fields differs from digital project to digital project, the following eight elements are always displayed directly below an image when viewed on the library's website:

1. Object title
2. Object description
3. Author/creator
4. Date scope
5. Subject keywords
6. Collections information (title of collection)
7. Publisher
8. Copyright statement

However, Historypin only displays primary information next to the image and any additional information, such as copyright statements and original links, are on a secondary display tab:

Primary display tab

1. Title

2. Date
3. Geographic location
4. Brief description
5. Tags

Secondary display tab

1. Copyright statement
2. Attribution
3. Author
4. Original link (original link of the digital collection)
5. Repository
6. Notes

Although UT Libraries and Historypin share a number of similar metadata elements, Historypin's display was an issue because it conflicted with a primary assessment priority: creating an access point to the original image for usage statistics. Because of its placement in the secondary tab, we weren't sure if every user would know to click there to find the original link that was covered by Google Analytics. To address this issue, we used UT Libraries' link shortener to create truncated web addresses for the original object URLs and inserted these at the top of the brief description field for enhanced visibility. This ensured available access back to the original image for usage statistics.

The second challenge was using geographic metadata with the pinning tool. Many of the images selected for ingestion did not have associated geographic information, however this was a mandatory metadata field. If items were not pinned to a location, content remained unpublished and invisible to the user. As a result, the majority of the location information needed to be added to the existing metadata, which required additional time when pinning content. To pin an image to a map for a regular collection, you enter the address into the map's search interface, and the software attempts to identify the location in Google Maps. However, in most cases, the results were close but not entirely accurate, which required us to fix each pin by scrolling through the map and finding the most accurate location. This process was even more comprehensive when using Google Street View to line up a historic image with the current view to create a mashup effect. To line up the images, we had to manually click through the Google Street View maps with their directional tools until we reached the desired location for each individual item. We then had to manipulate the street view to align each angle of the view to match the historic image.

Overall, ingestion of images and descriptive information for Historypin was not resource heavy, and we found almost all of our staff time was dedicated to pinning content and reformatting metadata to display properly for each individual item. Historypin does have the capability to batch-upload content, but it requires the creation of a separate metadata spreadsheet. Unless the content manager has technical experience exporting descriptive metadata from an original source, such as Archivists' Toolkit, utilizing the batch-uploader tool would still require staff time to copy and paste information for each item, including location information. Also, the batch-uploader tool does not allow for batch-uploading of location data, which is required for pinning. Adding geographic information to each image has to be done individually. For this reason, we chose not to use the tool.

One of Historypin's main attractions was its support for creating virtual tours featuring pinned images and descriptions in a sequence that is designed to tell a story. The process of creating a tour in Historypin is fairly simple once the images have been uploaded and described. The added steps involve ordering the selected images in a meaningful sequence and pinning historic images to align with a current image of that location via Google Street View. When Google Street View is available, the pinned image appears in a layer over the current Google Street View scene. Using a slider tool to make the historical image more or less opaque reveals the current street view image underneath, creating a mashup effect that allows users to see historical change by viewing the past in the present.

The material that best lent itself to the tour feature was a collection of historic campus images because of its focus on the university, the availability of exact physical addresses, and the number of Google Street Views of campus buildings. The "University of Tennessee, Knoxville Campus—Now and Then" tour we created features several images of iconic buildings on campus through time, flanked by descriptive text boxes that include: the date of the building, cost, architects, and/or some featured facts about the naming or the purpose for which the building was constructed (see figure 5.1).[8]

After we finished building our Historypin collections, we shifted our focus toward Pinterest, using material that was already digitized.[9] However, because the platform's metadata elements were limited to a title and brief description, which is truncated on the main page and only displays in its entirety when users select an individual pin, we used content that could stand alone with little or no description. Like Historypin, a field for linking back to the original image is embedded in the image after content is uploaded; clicking on the enlarged image automatically takes the user back to the originating site. As with Historypin, we used collections that were already popular and created the following boards: UT History, UT Football Programs, Alan Heilman Botanical Photographs, Early Images of Egypt, and Charlie Daniel Editorial Cartoons (see figure 5.2).

Content was uploaded every two weeks, and each board was updated at least once a month. The Pinterest boards were implemented and maintained by two staff members. For the initial phase, a total of 40 hours was

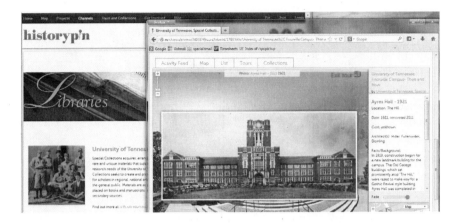

Figure 5.1.   A screenshot showing the Library's Historypin homepage on the left, and one of the buildings from our tour, "University of Tennessee, Knoxville Campus—Now and Then." Using the "Fade" feature at the bottom right users can gradually switch between our historic image and a current Google Street View image of the same building today

required to ingest 430 pins, or 5.6 minutes per image. Pinning content required minimal time; the majority of staff time was allocated to researching, selecting, and scanning content for the boards. Using the same average salary of $18 per hour, the total cost is $720 dollars, or approximately or $1.67 per item.

The primary challenge of working with Pinterest was not the pinning process or the administrator interface but the necessity to continually generate new content. Unlike Historypin, Pinterest creates the opportunity for more a consistent interaction between content and the user through likes, repins, and comments, providing administrators with useful and immediate feedback. As a result we changed our selection process from maintaining collections similar to those ingested in Historypin—based on already digitized material—to selecting content driven by user feedback. Thus, while the first Pinterest boards were representative of current digital collections, subsequent boards were developed based on perceived users' preferences that were gathered through their interactions with the content we pinned, particularly for materials related to the University of Tennessee, the East Tennessee geographic region, and southern and pop culture.

RESULTS

The primary research goals of the project were to determine if social media sites increased the discovery of and access to traditional digital collections and to assess the return on investment and long-term feasibil-

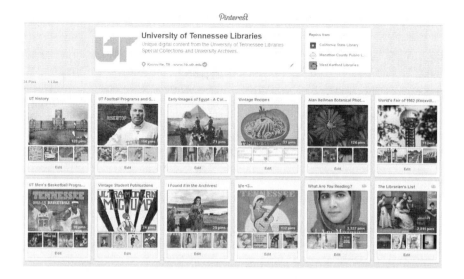

Figure 5.2. The Library's Pinterest homepage, showing our most recent collection of boards.

ity of using Web 2.0 tools to promote special collections material. One of the reasons we chose Historypin and Pinterest was that both platforms included built-in assessment metrics to help us measure the level of outreach we were achieving with our project. Historypin provides account administrators with basic metrics to guide the management of their content, primarily a simple metric called "views." The views metric allows account administrators to see how many times an image has been viewed on Historypin since it was uploaded. This metric includes not only unique visits but also repeat visits by the same user. Currently, this is Historypin's only available metric related to access and discoverability, therefore as a standalone measurement, this tool can only address simple queries based on comparative image or collection views. Using Google Analytics as a supplemental tool allows site administrators to compare usage data between the material on UT Libraries' website and the content in Historypin.

For the project, assessment was limited to the initial sample group of images ingested into Historypin from the project's implementation eight months prior. Compiled data showed that the images in this group were accessed an average of 22.4 times each via the nontraditional hosting platform Historypin. At first glance these numbers appear modest, but a comparative analysis to the same group of images hosted on the library website showed that the items were only accessed an average of 12.4 times.

Comparing access across collections in Historypin also revealed that certain types of images were better suited to the platform. Images from the Photographs of Tennessee Cities collection were accessed an average of 51.5 times each in Historypin, while they were only accessed approximately 6.3 times on the library's website. While this may seem surprising, the content of this collection might help explain its success in that these images document buildings and other architectural structures. As stated previously, images of specific locations are ideal for Historypin's map, street-view, and mashup functionality, as visual mashups allow users to compare historic buildings to their modern-day counterparts in real time. However, not all location-based collections were as successful. Images of landscapes were the least accessed overall, averaging just 13.2 views each. Still, these images had more unique visits on Historypin than via the library website (10.4 times each). In fact, every collection in the study was accessed more on average via Historypin than on the library website. In an effort to calculate how many users came back to our library website, we found that a total of 327 users, or an average of 3.8 per image, accessed our traditional website via Historypin.

When compared to Historypin, Pinterest provides more detailed analytics. Initially, the platform only provided the following metrics: followers, likes, repins, and comments. The followers metric refers to the total number of users that follow one or more of a poster's boards. When users choose to follow a board, they choose to receive all future pins from that board directly in their home pages. This helps users find new content that may interest them. The repins metric refers to the number of times users repinned an item to their own boards. By repinning an item, followers are sharing this item with their own followers and increasing the total number of individuals who see the pin. The likes metric refers to the number of users who have selected a pin to save and reference later. Finally, like Historypin, Pinterest users can comment on items.

With 14 boards, UT Libraries' Pinterest page had 430 posted pins and 303 unique followers over the first eight months the project. Four comments, 172 likes, and 654 repins account for the total number of end-user interactions. While the boards were started at different times, they have approximately the same number of followers. Each board, however, displays a different percentage of end-user interactions (percentages are based on the total number of pins versus the total number of interactions):

- Alan Heilman Botanical Photographs (27.9 percent liked; 304 percent repinned)
- Charlie Daniel Editorial Cartoons (6.7 percent liked; 50 percent repinned)
- Early Images of Egypt (71.4 percent liked; 125 percent repinned)

- I Found It in the Archives (186.7 percent liked; 473.3 percent re-pinned)
- The Throwback (66.7 percent liked; 233.3 percent repinned)
- UT History (25.9 percent liked; 187 percent repinned)
- UT Football Programs (31 percent liked; 166.7 percent repinned)
- UT Theatre Playbills (30 percent liked; 140 percent repinned)
- UT Men's Basketball Program (10 percent liked; 60 percent re-pinned)
- Vintage Recipes (12.5 percent liked; 62.5 percent repinned)
- Vintage Student Publications (0 percent liked; 40 percent repinned)
- We <3 (72.4 percent liked; 120.7 percent repinned)
- World's Fair, 1982 (45.4 percent liked; 209 percent repinned)

In reviewing the findings on user engagement, the boards with highest results were the ones with strong regional interest. Excluding a historic photograph of Elizabeth Taylor, the individual images that had the highest number of repins were early images of University of Tennessee campus buildings. This regional preference is also demonstrated on the "I Found It in the Archives" board. The few images that did not originate from UT Libraries' special collections materials are the only pins without any user interaction. Collectively, these numbers demonstrate that, while there are varying degrees of user interest in posted materials, users overwhelmingly prefer to engage with content through repinning. By liking an item, users only save an item for their own future use, while repinning allows users to share content with their followers. In regards to the relationship between our website and Pinterest, we found that a total of only thirty-six users directly accessed our website through Pinterest. This is likely due to the fact that Pinterest is a social site whose main purpose is content sharing.

This type of data is related to sociability and shareability only and does not provide information about findability or the access to and discovery of digital content. For example, Pinterest does not track the total number of times an image was accessed. However recent updates released in March 2013 have improved upon the previous scope of analytics tools. Instead of only tracking shareability and sociability metrics, Pinterest's enhanced assessment capability allows site administrators to track discovery and access of the posted content. These new metrics include: impressions, reach, clicks, and visitors. Impressions measures the total number of times a pin has been viewed, while reach is the number of unique users who view the content during a specific time period. By monitoring these two new metrics, site administrators can determine whether using this platform improves access and discovery of collection materials.

Because the enhanced assessment tools just recently became available, the case study was only able to compile a small sample of data. During a three-month period, a total of 232 images were added to Pinterest, and these items were viewed an average of 9 times each by 6 people. In this example, the impressions, or the average number of times an item was viewed, would be 9. The reach, or the number of unique users, would be 6. While this number may seem low, several factors can contribute to this result. Unlike Historypin, Pinterest users only tend to see content that has been recently posted. While Historypin leads users to discover new content by searching a map, Pinterest guides users to rely primarily on the user's home page. The layout of the home page is done chronologically, with the most recent pins from boards the user follows starting at the top. For this reason, when a user checks the home page, content that has been posted most recently is more likely to be discovered. The older the content is, the more difficult it may be to find. On Historypin, how recently an image was posted has no effect on the discovery of content. This can be even further complicated by the number of boards a user follows and how often he or she checks the site. Even if a user follows all the library's boards, he or she may never see any library content, depending on how many other boards that individual is following and when and how often they check the site. Because our plan was to upload content to Pinterest in batches on a biweekly basis, only our followers who logged in to the site around this time would see any new content. In retrospect, posting less content on a more frequent basis could have resulted in higher numbers of reach and impressions.

LESSONS LEARNED

Currently, UT Libraries uses Historypin to promote newly processed or heavily used archival collections; the amount of time to create a collection in Historypin is accounted for at the beginning of physical processing. While Historypin does make it fairly easy to upload information and pin new items, it does take quite a bit of time for a new user to master all the necessary functionalities. In our experience, it takes approximately five to ten hours of training for each new content manager. Due to time constraints, all student training is performed by one staff member, and usage of Historypin as a digital collections outreach tool is selective. The lesson here is to be aware of the time commitment Historypin requires and be selective with the collections you feature on the site so that the level of investment is warranted.

Another important lesson that we learned from Historypin was how to deal with the logistics of working with a third-party hosted site. The current iteration of Historypin is not a beta version, but it is still a work in progress. From an administrative standpoint, this means using workarounds to address platform functionality issues. For example, when the project first began, there was no way to create a unique link for a posted collection in the administrative interface. Despite the hierarchical arrangement of content within the page, the URL in the address bar remained the same. To get a unique URL, the administrator had to behave as a user and enter the Historypin site from the home page and search for the collection. However, there was not a search function for collection title at the time, so the desired collection had to be found by scrolling through a list of all hosted collections. The search function has been fixed, and the software is continually updated to address other functionality issues.

Historypin has been readily available to answer queries. We contacted their support team regarding the unique URL issue, and they let us know that this update was one of their priorities. We have continued to contact the organization to address any issues we have had and to keep up to date on forthcoming changes. However, being unable to directly change how a platform functions is a factor to keep in mind when considering software hosted by a third party.

Like Historypin, we have continued to use Pinterest, however our focus is primarily on topical interests and event-based outreach rather than marketing new collections. UT Libraries is currently hosting fourteen boards on its Pinterest page, such as the UT Theatre Playbills, Vintage Student Publications, and We <3. Based on our project findings, we are changing the process for posting new content. Because of new features included in the analytics console, it is now possible to determine how other users unaffiliated with the library are pinning site content and how their use affects access and discovery of digital collections. For example, the new "pins" and "pinners" metrics reveal the number of items that were pinned from the site and the unique pinners that were responsible. The "repins" and "repinners" metrics shows how often those pins were repinned and the unique users responsible. Finally and most importantly, the "clicks" and "visitors" metrics can be used to determine how Pinterest is improving access and discovery of pinned items. The former metric reports the number of times images that were taken from our website and added to Pinterest were seen on the site, while the latter defines the total amount of users who saw any of the content from our website via Pinterest. With the availability of this data, site administrators can fully determine what effects Pinterest has on overall discovery of digital collections.

Another change that will be implemented is how often content will be posted to Pinterest. While collecting content and limiting pinning to twice per month seemed reasonable in the beginning, a closer look at the project's final analytics and specific metrics revealed that discovery and access were not being increased as much as we had hoped. According to research from Pinerly and Bitly, the peak times to pin are 2:00 p.m. to 4:00 p.m. and 8:00 p.m. to 1:00 a.m. on weekdays and on Saturday mornings. [10] For this reason, during the next phase of the project, less content will be posted on a more frequent basis to reach a larger audience. In order to maximize staff time and take advantage of these peak hours, scheduling software will be used to automate pinning times and frequency. This change was minor because it did not affect how we were collecting materials to pin.

CONCLUSION

In evaluating the success of Historypin and Pinterest as marketing and outreach tools for our special collections material, we found that these channels both improved traffic to our digitized collection material and reached a broader audience than our traditional library websites. From these findings we feel that these two tools are worth incorporating into our digital processing and outreach strategies. While users of Historypin and Pinterest may find our special collections material for a variety of reasons, these sites are giving us additional means of reaching a broader audience than ever before. UT special collections is now incorporating Historypin into our processing workflow and is selectively using to it to promote newly processed collections. For example, we recently ingested several new collections into the platform, including albums of World War II images, African American history, and the Smoky Mountain region. Our findings have not changed how we use the platform, but because the statistics indicated a higher response to images related specifically to the Tennessee region or broader national themes, we try to keep our content within those topics.

To build on our lessons learned from Historypin and its mapping tool, our plan is to move forward in mapping our content to capitalize on the move toward augmented reality (AR) in mobile applications. AR allows the real-time viewing of physical spaces embedded with digital content.[11] For example, a user's mobile device can be pointed at building, and the layering of images of the same building from the past and information about it will become visible. In our case, we could use AR functionality to elevate the user's experience of our digital content in the campus tour from an interactive social media website to the real-world environment. For the next phase of this project, we are exploring the possibility of using the location-based app Layar, which directs users to nearby points of interest and allows them to access associated content, such as audio, video, images, and descriptive text.

We are also continuing to pin items to Pinterest. Images are selected in advance, and we use a spreadsheet to document where the image came from (a digital collection or a new scan), the board that it is being pinned to, and then the time it was uploaded. Based on our findings, we now only upload images between the peak times of 2:00 and 4:00 p.m. on weekdays using Pingraphy, a Pinterest scheduler, which automates the process.[12]

For this project we wanted to explore harnessing the power of social media platforms to enhance access and discovery of our special collections materials while also allowing users to create their own added value to our online content. While we planned for implementation and assessment, we did not have a strategy in place for long-term sustainability or modifying our use of social platforms to meet our objectives. For this case study, our project findings were useful in determining if and how social media can have an impact in promoting digital collections. For this data to prove meaningful, we have to not only incorporate what we have learned into our processes but also continuously assess the efficacy of our use of these tools as users' needs and content-hosting dynamics change. We plan to consistently monitor our use of and changes to these platforms and assess whether our endeavors in these areas are effective as part of our long-term strategy to continue exploring ways to meet users where they are.

*Mark Baggett is systems development librarian, **Rabia Gibbs** is manuscripts archivist, and **Alesha Shumar** is university archivist at the University of Tennessee, Knoxville.*

NOTES

1. Lev Manovich, *The Language of New Media* (Cambridge: MIT Press, 2002), 96.

2. "15 Most Popular Networking Sites: April 2013," *eBizMBA*, accessed April 19, 2013, http:// www.ebizmba.com/articles/social-networking-websites.

3. Alissa Skelton, "Social Demographics: Who's Using Today's Biggest Networks," *Mashable*, March 9, 2012, http://mashable.com/2012/03/09/social-media-demographics .

4. "Top Mashup Tags," *ProgrammableWeb*, accessed April 19, 2013, http://www. programmableweb.com/mashups.

5. While the tour feature was later used for a campus tour to layer historic building images over current locations, the street view functionality was not implemented for the beginning of the project, as the majority of the images were interior shots or originated from more regional non–address-specific locations.

6. "What Are Tours?" *Historypin*, accessed April 14, 2013, http://www.historypin. com/tours/all.

7. "The University of Tennessee, Special Collections," *Historypin*, accessed April 14, 2013, http://www.historypin.com/channels/view/34019/#!photos/list.

8. "University of Tennessee, Knoxville Campus—Then and Now," *Historypin*, accessed October 13, 2013, http://www.historypin.com/channels/view/34019/#!tours/view/id/1789/title/University%20of%20Tennessee%2C%20Knoxville%20Campus-%20Then%20and%20Now.

9. "University of Tennessee Libraries," *Pinterest*, accessed October 13, 2013, http:// pinterest.com/utklibraries .

10. Krissy Brady, "The Best and Worst Times to Post on Social Networks," *Social Caffeine*, July 2012, http://lorirtaylor.com/the-best-and-worst-times-to-post-on-social-networks-infographic.

11. Augmented reality (AR) projects digital content onto a real-world setting. The average user most frequently interacts with AR content through mobile apps.

12. Note that Pingraphy is now Viraltag, http://www.pingraphy.com.

SIX

Creating a New Learning Center

Designing a Space to Support Multiple Outreach Goals

Dorothy Dougherty,
National Archives at New York City

When the National Archives at New York City relocated to the Alexander Hamilton U.S. Custom House at One Bowling Green in late 2012, it was a chance to create—from the ground up—a learning center that would establish programming and outreach as a central part our region's mission. Building the learning center provided a unique opportunity to establish a distinct space for outreach and discovery, a feature lacking in our previous location on Varick Street, just two miles away. Because we were relocating to an area of the city popular with tourists from all over the world and New York natives alike, we could promote an understanding and appreciation for the National Archives to millions of people with broad interests, such as U.S. history or immigration, in addition to smaller populations of repeat visitors with interests specific to our holdings, such as New York federal court records or Ellis Island passenger manifests.

The new space at the Custom House was an extraordinary opportunity, but in planning our programs, we still faced a familiar problem: limited space. Our challenge was to create the one-room learning center as a multifunctional space that could accommodate a variety of programs and audiences with different needs and interests. Our vision was not only to provide preregistered workshops and programs but also to create a new visitor experience for self-directed learning. The learning center at Custom House would become a hands-on discovery room. We first had to determine the specific functions we wanted for the space and then design an effective space to support those functions. A small team, mainly based in New York, who helped conceptualize the space, did our overall project planning. Like any project we strived to work as efficiently as possible within our given budget and put together the right team to help us brainstorm and develop our ideas and design for our space. Ultimately, with thoughtful planning, inspired collaboration, determined persistence, and last-minute good luck, we created a space where visitors could connect to the archives in memorable and unexpected ways.

PLANNING

Before moving to the Custom House, all the operations of the National Archives at New York City had been housed in a nondescript federal building in the West Village of Manhattan. Access to our office was less than optimal and the first hurdle to our outreach efforts. The Varick Street location was limiting for a number of reasons. Even though the building housed other federal offices, their visitors consisted primarily of persons seeking passports or summoned to court for immigration-related issues. The building itself was not designed to accommodate a high volume of people or drop-in visitation. Its entrance and lobby were much like any city office building. A generic dull lobby sign, easily overlooked, and a standard listing on the building directory were the only indications that this was, in fact, the location of the archives. We were not even permitted to place a "National Archives" sign on the façade, which meant visitation was limited to intrepid researchers and program participants. As a result, we provided mostly seasonal programming for our audience attendees, including genealogists, educators, and a limited number of students. Our public programs largely served a small core group, with many repeat attendees who knew the intricacies of the building and had the fortitude to seek us out.

Despite this less-than-optimal arrangement (perhaps *because* of this less-than-optimal arrangement), we worked hard to establish our programs and build a loyal visitor base. Clearly, a move from Varick Street could only improve our situation, but at the same time, we wanted to maintain continuity for our programs and not risk losing that audience base in the process. We also wanted our visitors to have an improved level of access to archival records and research. This access would greatly extend the relevance and service of the National Archives to the public. The Custom House at One Bowling Green is a building that was open to walk-in visitation and could accommodate a high volume of visitors. It is situated next to Battery Park in lower Manhattan, where tourists depart for the Statue of Liberty and Ellis Island, just blocks from Ground Zero.[1] These nationally significant attractions see millions of visitors each year.

The Custom House was constructed on the same location as the first Dutch settlements, and throughout our nation's history, the area has been a focal point of maritime activity, as it is bordered by the East River and the Hudson River. The building itself served as the Custom House for many years, with its story revealed within our many National Archives holdings. Today, the Customs Service is located elsewhere, and the building has become a public attraction due to efforts by the Smithsonian Institution's popular Museum of the American Indian, which operates free to the public year round. Generally, people visiting this area tend to be interested in history; they come to these places to connect with a national consciousness and to historic events that they or their families may have a personal connection with. They are ideal candidates for a new wave of walk-in and potentially repeat visitors to the National Archives at New York.

We were offered space along the third-floor corridor at the Custom House, which is where we would provide our public access to the welcome, learning, and research centers, with staff offices on the fourth floor. As an archive our priority is to expand researcher access. The new research center would allow research services to double the number of public access computers they had at Varick Street.

The prospect of designing a new outreach space housed within this high-profile location was very exciting. In planning our new outreach space, we faced the same question all archives do, big and small: How do you get people interested in records? From years of programming feedback, we knew the public wanted to engage directly with our holdings. It was also our experience that, by developing a level of interaction that is both educational and personal, people respond with a high level of engagement, curiosity, surprise, and understanding. Our goal at the learning center was to instill that experience in all visitors, whether they are students, educators, researchers, tourists, preregistered patrons, or simply walk-in visitors.

Because our vision for the learning center was for this variety of offerings and audiences, to be an effective multifunctional space, we needed to clearly articulate these needs—and champion our vision. It was a major challenge in the first step of planning. As the move and construction team leader for our office, I oversaw defining the functional and conceptual needs of our new spaces. I was fortunate to pull into the New York City planning team NARA's national museum coordinator from Washington, DC, Lisa Royse, as well as our New York–based education specialist Chris Zarr and education technician Sara Lyons Davis for ongoing brainstorming meetings. The assistant regional administrator, Dave Powers, located in Boston yet overseeing the New York construction project, was instrumental in helping us with our planning.

Our architects suggested we focus the center on one purpose. That is, they recommended we make it a classroom or a lecture hall or a discovery room but not try to serve all those purposes with one space. However, our planning team felt it needed to be more than just one type of space because limiting it meant we would miss key opportunities for family outreach and drop-in visitation. Our objectives were to expand and improve our public outreach and to attract and serve a broad and varied public audience in our new location. If we developed the space correctly, multiple functions could work. The next challenge was how to accomplish this. By limiting programs to set times, such as the morning, we could establish a new target audience for afternoon unstructured walk-ins. Both educator and student workshops worked well in the mornings because it met professional development requirements during core hours and students could travel both to and from the archives, with enough time for lunch and to return to school in time for dismissal. We also had a legacy of success with lunchtime genealogy workshops, so we knew that time frame worked for that type of program.

Defining the outreach programs for walk-ins with no specific intent or expectation about the National Archives was our next consideration. We wanted to engage the public with elements that may spark in them an interest to begin family history research and further explore our records. There could also be crossover interests from Museum of the American Indian visitors seeking to learn about relevant Native American records in the archives. The question was: How do we reach a broad and diverse visitor population that *may* have heard of the National Archives in Washington, DC, but most likely never heard of the National Archives in New York and therefore had no expectation or desire to see it? We were not willing to give up on attracting these kinds of new visitors in our space and limit the function of the room to just visitors who already knew who we were. Just as the National Archives is committed to serving the needs of the entire public, we were committed to making our one space work for everyone who came through our doors.

We solicited feedback from our counterparts who had developed the Boeing Learning Center at the National Archives in Washington, DC; brainstormed internally about current programming, new programming, and best practices; and even took a few benchmarking trips to area institutions to see how they treated "learning" spaces.[2] Our DC counterparts who participated in the creation of the Boeing Learning Center made a simple key suggestion: Write down your goals. In retrospect, maybe this should have been an obvious first step, but it was something that we hadn't taken the time to do. Once we sat down and defined them, our goals were simple—to provide engaging outreach experiences for multiple audiences with a variety of programs, including:

- scheduling formal programs for preregistered attendees, including educators, students, genealogists, professional associations/organizations, federal agencies, etc.

- establishing informal discovery sessions for individual, group, and family walk-in visitors
- continuing outreach to our core audience and expand offerings to the general public, especially individuals touring the downtown area
- delivering a memorable experience to engage visitors with the holdings of the National Archives in a learning center

Outlining these goals in a formal white paper helped us articulate to the architects specific requirements for the room, as well as the IT and electrical needs, and identify programmatic materials for development. For example, with morning programs we needed to determine the number of tables and chairs to purchase, their layout, placement of the main desk, choice of a projection screen or smart board or both, wireless access, and computer access. The considerations were many, and ultimately the rationale behind our final selections was determined by our budget and what we already knew from our current programming.

In analyzing the needs of our current programming, first we considered the average size of our preregistered groups. Because the average New York City school class is roughly thirty-five students, we needed space large enough to accommodate that target group plus several chaperones, so tables and chairs for roughly forty people would suffice. We then needed to consider if the layout should be set up as a classroom or lecture style because that would determine the type of furniture we purchased, especially because collapsible tables and stackable chairs could also be easily moved and stored. Would staff have to move and set up or break down the tables for each type of program? Was there other space in the building we could host lectures in if necessary? After investigating options for use of other building rooms for large lectures, we learned that there was an auditorium we could use that would seat up to three hundred people. With this in mind, we decided the learning center would be set up as a classroom and worked with a furniture designer to purchase stationary tables, which were sturdier and fit the room's aesthetic better than the collapsible ones.

Although it may seem like a minor issue, there was debate between choosing round tables or square. Square tables could be lined up and reshape the layout of the room. Round tables were more inviting but gave us less flexibility. After considering each option and consequence of it, we chose inviting, smaller round tables because that served the majority of our program needs.

We also needed to consider the IT capabilities of the room. Based on our teacher workshops, including our all-day symposiums, we knew many educators bring their laptops, so we installed wireless Internet access. Our smart board, while small for large workshop viewing, would work for our teacher programs. We realized that we also needed a larger projection screen for our genealogy programs and other large-group presentations, so we ordered the larger screen.

In thinking about programs for our self-directed audiences — the informal walk-in visitor — we had a rare opportunity to deliver the unexpected and unanticipated. To build upon the national program, the learning center took elements from the National Archives' resource room in Washington, DC, where visitors are encouraged to freely "pull" archival records for themselves and participate in a kind of "archivist/researcher role play" in which they discover a variety of thematic-based records. By simulating the archivist-researcher experience, we model the mission of the National Archives in providing access to records that document our rights as American citizens, the actions of federal officials, and our own national experience.[3] Another element that originated in the DC resource room is "Archival Adventures," a self-directed activity that is essentially a guided research query about a popular or historically significant record. In New York we place the majority of our facsimiles in archival boxes on shelves for the public to pull down. We broadened the "Archival Adventures" activity to require users to open an "adventure box," examine the contents of a folder, and answer questions about its contents. Each document has additional related documents within the folder to show how records are connected and how research builds upon multiple findings. It is a simple and fun way of engaging the public in research activity without the perception of conducting laborious research.

IMPLEMENTATION

Once we identified our goals and worked out the details of our requirements, we were ready to move into the construction phase and begin working on implementing our ideas. As we sought to connect visitors to history, we encouraged the architectural and construction firm to work with the historical integrity of the Custom House and bring to the learning center elements representational of the Beaux Arts building.[4] Because the project involved a grant for historic rehabilitation, the historic wall trim was uncovered, and wood floors were replaced; the drop ceiling was removed to expose twelve-foot-high ceilings. The firm added large chandelier lighting in the center of the room to reflect a turn-of-the-century charm. Our budget for the project only included the architecture design and structural build-out of the space, so we added as many design elements as possible to the build-out of the space. For example, we asked the architects to custom-build a bookcase that would house our archival boxes, a map cabinet to store additional oversize facsimiles, cabinets for storage, and a main desk as part of construction. Completing these large-ticket and necessary items during the construction phase helped us save money for a future graphic design treatment to brand the learning center.

We finalized the functional requirements by considering every programmatic scenario and its supportive elements. Essentially all our programs would be interactive, encourage participants to access records within the archival boxes on the shelves, and possibly view learning activities or presentations on our whiteboard or screen. We considered every way the room would be used. A student field trip, grades 4 through 12, for example, focuses on our New York designed document analysis workshop, "Hands-on Archives." Students are asked to make connections between their lives and the experiences of those who came before them by examining a selection of facsimile materials. Worksheets guide students from one record to the next in a collaborative research simulation. In this scenario the classroom would need to be set up to facilitate engagement, therefore the tables would need to accommodate this collaboration and hold the related tools of the program, such as magnifying glasses, white gloves, archival boxes, and pencils (see figure 6.1).

A second scenario of how the learning center would be used was one of educator engagement for instructors of grades 4 through 12. Educators would analyze documents, make connections between their Common Core curriculum requirements, learn how to "teach with documents" from the National Archives, and participate in a space that connects them

Figure 6.1. View of the Learning Center, showing the built-in bookcases and storage features. In the foreground is one of our subject-themed archival boxes, which visitors can "pull" off the shelf during self-discovery sessions.

with other educators. Additional activities would incorporate smart-board demonstrations of DocsTeach,[5] document facsimiles, and National Archive online resources. Modeling student document analysis activities, small- and large-group discussions, and collaborative lesson development meant we had to ensure the right space layout for that engagement.

Other scenarios of use we considered were our lunchtime "Finding Family" genealogy workshops, historical lectures, author events, panel discussions, and symposia. In these structured, large-audience programs, visibility of the projection screen was crucial, as was access to program-themed facsimile records in our archival boxes. These program attendees often take notes and bring their lunches, so the classroom-style table layout worked. The final scenario was a brand new functionality for us— the afternoon walk-in visitor. We had to visualize how activities would work with the setup and materials we were planning to use. Any activity that included easy self-discovery to our materials on the bookcase would work. Again the classroom layout suited this type of program activity, as it provided close proximity to the shelf of historical records, a crucial element for engagement.

As these scenarios played out, we confirmed that the bookcase for our archival boxes was a main attraction to visitors and a primary point of engagement in experiencing the archives' records. We figured the bookcase could house additional program materials and include cubbies for worksheets, handouts, and storage of our portable magnifying glasses and pencil caddies. Our team then needed to determine how we wanted to organize the archival boxes—thematically, chronologically, or by lesson plan. Selecting content for the boxes was yet another challenge. We wanted to include content that related to themes of the city, our historic building, and the U.S. Custom Service, as well as tie into our partners and other area cultural institutions. We also solicited additional records from our regional and DC counterparts to make our final selections.

We ordered furniture to fit the overall simplicity of the room and bridged modern furniture style with the historical backdrop of the space. With our furniture budget, we could also further enhance the look of the space. Our furniture consultant suggested a pop of color with dark blue chairs contrasted by light wooden round tables to play off the light-colored wood floors. We included as much technical requirements into the construction as we could. We asked for as many power outlets as possible, several computer drops, and wireless access and determined placement of the projector and screen, location of the smart board, and area for a printer. We visited the space to make sure the drawings accurately reflected our desired plan. What would the visitors' first impressions be? What would draw people into the room? What would they see first? If the main attraction was the records, then the archival bookcase/map cabinet needed to be placed within view of the doorway. We had addressed all our functional requirements and even tied a few design elements into that function. What we really needed was to transform the room beyond architecture and furniture into a graphically designed space that branded the room as the National Archives learning center.

We were thrilled when the Foundation for the National Archives committed to support the graphic design phase.[6] The space was already planned out, but aside from the bookcase, furniture, and white walls, there was no unique aesthetic that branded the learning center with its own look and feel. Funding from the foundation gave us the chance to hire an exhibit designer,[7] bring cohesion to the learning center by introducing graphics and images from our holdings on the wall, and finish the space with a look appropriate for the National Archives.

We had already built the bookcase at the entryway of the space to showcase our archival "discovery" boxes. We wanted to further show people we are a repository of records, so we worked very closely with our graphic designer to brainstorm how key, high-profile documents in all types of media (e.g., textual handwritten or typed documents, photographs, charts, drawings, architectural drawings, posters) could demonstrate the wide variety of materials the archives safeguards for the public. At this stage we had very specific ideas about what we wanted. We wanted an appropriate space that was engaging for all ages, not too young and not wholly academic. We wanted the documents to speak for themselves in all their diversity. We learned that words in a graphic treatment would be a less obtrusive design and less expensive and were encouraged to consider this approach. However, the archivist in me felt the records had to be true to form; that is, we wanted to show the records themselves and not crop them for design purposes. We also didn't want the space to look like a gallery. We needed to make sure people knew this was a place to interact with and engage with records, not just look at them. Our designer was instrumental in strategically placing the images in a way that piqued the interest of anyone coming into the space; it was clear that this is not a gallery of images but a space overflowing with records ready to be discovered (see figure 6.2).

We brainstormed heavily about this selection of images for the space and considered themed walls at first. We also considered our most requested and popular holdings. Ultimately we wanted a variety: significant documents from our nationwide holdings, New York–specific materials, popular ones, some of our personal favorites, and a variety of record types (e.g., textual, graphic, architectural, etc.). We made a list of our "must haves" and then other possibilities. Our designer helped us choose the best visual representation. When we shared our learning center mission statement with him, he helped us to make another connection. To conceptually link the public with the documents, he suggested we incorporate magnetic walls as part of the design, using star- and arrow-shaped magnets to attach and therefore call out a document as being significant in some way (see figure 6.3). Visitors could locate an

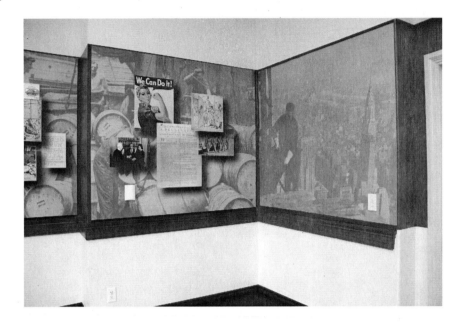

Figure 6.2.   A view of the walls of the Learning Center showing the implementation of the images selected for our graphic design.

"interesting" or "favorite" record and add it to the wall with a magnet. This personal experience mimics an "archival" action people do almost every day at home when they select an important piece of paper, photo, or drawing and attach it to the kitchen refrigerator or bulletin board with a magnet, pin, or tape. We were excited to incorporate this element into the design.

With foundation funding we were able to purchase a quality copier so visitors could take home copies of documents. Another "take away" they funded were souvenir magnets that read "I Connected to History at the National Archives at New York City." Now we were on a roll and began considering the pie-in-the-sky options. As a trained archivist, my personal view on the physical archival box was of all the interesting, exciting things waiting to be discovered inside a box. With that in mind, I proposed custom-designing archival boxes adorned with colorful graphics linked to the ones found in our space. These boxes help convey the breadth of content within our holdings. We designed a portable cart to set up impromptu discovery session stations outside our space in the building lobby and rotunda that showcased selected documents for people visiting the building to discover. We were fortunate that the foundation stepped in and provided the funding that helped realize the full potential of the space.

Figure 6.3. Copies of documents, attached to the wall with red star and yellow arrow magnets.

RESULTS

To help promote our new home in the Custom House, the National Archives at New York City held a major partner event in October 2012. We worked with the foundation and internal communication department to generate media interest, which allowed us to be featured in a number of articles, on a local TV spot, and in social media posts. Just days later, Hurricane Sandy hit the New York metropolitan area and caused construction delays. This pushed back our official opening to February 2013. In our first eight months of operation, we have been very busy with ongoing programs, educational workshops, and student field trips, reaching more than 10,000 visitors to our welcome center and providing 68 programs to 2,274 on-site attendees. In comparison to visitor statistics from the same period at our old location one year earlier, we have more than tripled our outreach. So far the learning center has been most popular with our preregistered visitors. Staff host morning and full-day professional development sessions for teachers and students. We found the teachers love that moment of discovery when opening archival boxes on our shelves and making multiple copies to take home to use in their classrooms. Student field trips have been very well received and provide students with a memorable experience of exploring archival records in an archival box. The room's interactivity has also been incorporated into programs: students star (with a magnet) interesting documents on the wall, teachers pull records off the shelf, and people happily take away our souvenir magnets. In just six months, we have used a full set of toner for the printer and exhausted our magnet supply. Additionally a number of genealogy and "Introduction to the National Archives" sessions have occurred in the space for small groups. Building up our program for preregistered programs has been a priority for the first year.

We found the overall layout works well for the increased number of walk-in visitors coming to the learning center. The archival boxes are an immediate draw. By labeling select boxes with themes, attendees know which boxes to open and explore based on their interests. Staff also put boxes out on the tables as well as some oversize records, which create another immediate attraction for the public. They will sit down, some-time stay a long while, often ask questions, profess their delight and amazement, and thank us. Having computers readily accessible provides another level of access to our online resources. Having the opportunity to build out a learning center in New York helped us bridge elements of our DC educational program to locations beyond the DC area. By doing this we continue a national model that seeks to reach across the country, serving multiple and diverse audiences, such as the New York metropolitan area.

LESSONS LEARNED

None of the members of our team had been through a design and construction project of this kind, and we certainly learned many lessons from our experience. First, we found it was extremely important to write goals down to finalize our vision. This helped frame our direction for the architects, furniture designer, and graphic designer. Communication was equally important, especially because people interpreted goals in different ways. Ongoing dialogue was crucial at every stage, helped prevent costly changes at late stages, and enabled us to make the best-informed decisions possible.

We found we could build on lessons learned and best practices from similar projects and modify them to create a unique experience for our space. Equally important was a supportive and committed team to help facilitate the desired outcome. A solid team that is motivated, flexible, responsive, and able to meet tight deadlines can mean the difference between a good plan and an awesome plan. A good team is willing to go the extra mile, review every aspect of the plan, continually brainstorm, share ideas, and actively play out or model every scenario in detail. And because all plans must come to an end, a good team also knows when to accept that the plan is complete and move toward implementation.

We kept costs down by buying items off the shelf, which in turn freed up funds to customize unique items for our space. For example, students need a place for their lunchboxes and jackets, but we didn't want to give up real estate for lockers, so we purchased wheeled see-through bins that easily stacked in our storage closet when not in use. This enabled us to spend money designing archival outreach boxes to brand our activity and create another feature for the room.

Another way we stretched our budget was to incorporate furniture into the design, as we did in having built-in bookshelves. We also kept the design costs low by doing the majority of the legwork in advance, for example, outlining goals, choosing records to showcase, and scanning high-resolution files so our designer didn't have to do all that work. As a result we saved time and money and were able to meet very tight deadlines. We also tried to be conservative with our use of technology. We wanted to bring users back to the traditional research method—that is, to examine documents in their hands, up close. We did make sure we could provide access to supportive online resources to enhance—but only to enhance, not detract from—the hands-on experience.

CONCLUSION

Although our budget and opportunities were beyond those of most archives, the challenge we faced in designing the learning center is a common one: creating a space that conveys the organization's mission. Whether you are building a new space, refurbishing a current space, or just engaging in a new outreach goal, it is important to determine the most effective representation of your repository. We understood that many people don't know what the National Archives is and that we had an opportunity to use the design of this new space as an extension of our outreach to engage users with the records and build that understanding. Having the opportunity and budget to do this was a once-in-a-lifetime opportunity for the New York staff.

Once we actually wrote out our goals for the learning center, it helped identify the required functional elements that the design would support. Even though the architects initially didn't understand what we wanted and why, we felt it was imperative to stay true to our vision of developing a multifunctional outreach space. We knew that our current programming (basically preregistered programs) would function much better in our new center; we knew the addition of a new outreach experience— that of walk-in visitors—was a key target in our new location. The enhancement of foundation funding created additional opportunities for branded design and brought focus to the need for an ongoing investment in the space. We feel we have created the best space possible as a result.

We recently began conversations to finalize a permanent exterior and interior "way-finding" plan to increase visitation into our spaces. In the meantime we bring our "discovery outreach cart" into the main lobby of the building and find it directly increases visitation into the learning center, demonstrating a need for better building signage.

While at times the process was overwhelming, it was completely rewarding. Knowing what you don't know is as central to planning as is finding the right support network. While we expected a learning curve during the first year of operation, tweaks needed to the space have been minor, and the learning center continues to allow us to reach more and more of the public.

Dorothy Dougherty received her master's degree in history with an archives certificate from C. W. Post, Long Island University. She was formerly a Manhattan research consultant, New York State Archives records manager, and historical museum interpreter. She is currently the programs director at the National Archives at New York City.

NOTES

1. "Alexander Hamilton U.S. Custom House, New York, NY," *U.S. General Services Administration*, accessed October 25, 2013, http://www.gsa.gov/portal/ext/html/site/hb/category/25431/actionParameter/exploreByBuilding/buildingId/644.

2. "The Boeing Learning Center," *U.S. National Archives*, accessed October 25, 2013, http://www.archives.gov/education/student-visits/dc.html.

3. "About the National Archives," *National Archives*, accessed October 25, 2013, http://www.archives.gov/about. View links for the complete mission and vision statements as well as the most recent strategic plan.

4. Wank Adams Slavin Associates, LLP, (WASA, http://www.wasallp.com). WASA was the architectural and engineering firm awarded the building design contract for the National Archives space at the U.S. Custom House.

5. "DocsTeach," *National Archives*, accessed October 25, 2013, http://docsteach.org . See also Stephanie Greenhut and Suzanne Isaacs, "DocsTeach.org: The Archives Offers Teachers New Tools to Stir Student Interest in History," *Prologue Magazine* 42, no. 3 (Fall 2010), http://www.archives.gov/publications/prologue/2010/fall/docsteach.html.

6. "Foundation for the National Archives," *National Archives*, accessed October 25, 2013, http://www.archives.gov/nae/support. The foundation is an independent 501(c)(3) nonprofit organization that since 1992 has served as the National Archives' private partner in introducing new audiences to the educational power of original records. The Foundation for the National Archives works in partnership with the National Archives to "open the stacks" of the archives and enable millions of visitors to interact personally with the original records of our democracy.

7. Roger Westerman Designs, LLC, was awarded the graphic design contract for graphic design treatment of the learning center and welcome center. Examples of his work are found at http://westermandesign.com. A subcontract of this work was awarded to Kearney and Associates (http://www.kearneyassoc.com) for fabrication and built out of the actual components, such as the wall treatment and graphics for the learning space.

SEVEN

"Wikipedia Is Made of People!"

Revelations from Collaborating with the World's Most Popular Encyclopedia

Sara Snyder, Archives of American Art

Over the last several years, a number of libraries and archives, including the Smithsonian Institution's Archives of American Art, have turned their attention to how Wikipedia can help increase access to our collections. Projects to add links to archival sources in Wikipedia are increasingly reported in the professional literature.[1] What makes the Archives of American Art's approach innovative is the way that we have shifted our focus from adding links to becoming active members of the global Wikipedia community. Today, instead of simply adding information ourselves, we are harnessing the power of the community to share the archives' resources on our behalf. What began as a rather unsophisticated mass linking scheme in 2007 has evolved into a new way of thinking about how our digital collections might serve the public. By encouraging and empowering Wikipedia volunteers (a.k.a., "Wikipedians") to make use of our resources, providing outreach and training for new editors, and incentivizing improvement of neglected articles and topics, we have created an ongoing program that benefits the archives and researchers alike.

This case study highlights the Archives of American Art's history of working with Wikipedia from 2007 to the present, including hosting our first Wikipedian in residence. It documents our gradual evolution in focus from "How can Wikipedia benefit the archives?" to "How can we help make Wikipedia a better reference work to the benefit of researchers, students, and lifelong learners?"

PLANNING

Imagine the repository where you work holds the papers of the somewhat obscure (but terribly important in her field) Jane Doe. Her collection has an excellent finding aid and lots of digitized material, yet when you Google her, the very first result—the one that around half of all people click on—is not the finding aid to her collection but her Wikipedia biography. Shouldn't that article include information about Doe's papers in your archives?

This is the logic that led to the Archives of American Art's first experiments editing Wikipedia in 2007. That August, an intern was sent to English Wikipedia with instructions to add links to relevant holdings in our collections from a list of artists' biography pages. She registered an account called "Aaa intern"—a username that, we later learned, violated Wikipedia's policy against shared institutional accounts and fairly screamed "conflict of interest." Within days, the intern had added links to collection record URLs in the "External Links" section of more than a hundred Wikipedia articles. Almost just as quickly, to our dismay, administrators flagged her account for spamming and blocked her from making further edits.

Are links to archival resources really spam? We did not know the answer, and in fact the Wikipedia community was at that moment debating the question intensely among themselves, as Michele Combs has documented.[2] Several editors attempted to reach out to "Aaa intern" on her Wikipedia talk page, but because back then nobody at the Archives of American Art understood how talk pages worked, we missed the opportunity to pursue the conversation.[3] Here is an example of a message that was posted:

> *Please Stop*
> Could you please stop adding external links for the moment and join in on a discussion that has been opened on *WT:WPSPAM*? . . . It may very well be that the links you are adding are appropriate, but the way you are adding them is in conflict with our guidelines on conflict of interest, spam, and possibly external links. Thanks.—Dirk Beetstra 14:46, 4 September 2007 (UTC)

In fact, the Wikipedia editors ultimately concluded that the intern account should be unblocked. They even pasted a full "Guide to Using Citations" on her talk page, but by then the archives' staff had been frightened off and instructed the intern to abandon the project. I continued making small edits to a few dozen artists' pages under my own individually registered Wikipedia account (User:Sarasays), adding links to relevant finding aids and oral history interviews, as did a member of our cataloging staff, but always with a sense of caution. After that first accusation of spamming, I was not sure if content from the archives was welcome on Wikipedia.

Thankfully, the tone and precedent for interaction between cultural institutions and Wikipedians was to change a few short years later. In the summer of 2010, the British Museum hosted the first Wikipedian in residence, Liam Wyatt, a Wikipedia administrator from Australia. Wyatt partnered with the institution to help share its educational resources and expertise with Wikipedia's immense audience.[4] The global Wikimedia community was inspired and invigorated by Wyatt's success and by the British Museum's openness and receptivity to a partnership.

That summer, buoyed by the developments at the British Museum, a group of Washington, DC–based Wikipedia volunteers reached out to some Smithsonian staff members; they organized an in-person training and information session for the staff. I attended this event along with a range of colleagues, from IT staff to curators to museum educators, all of whom received instructions on registering a Wikipedia account and understanding how to avoid conflict-of-interest issues.[5]

This encouragement from the Wikipedians was the signal the Archives of American Art had been waiting for. We were finally getting a clear message that institutional contributions from galleries, libraries, archives, and museums (in Wiki parlance, "GLAMs") are, in fact, welcome and encouraged in Wikipedia. Since 2010, the global GLAM-Wiki initiative has gone on to help cultural institutions around the world share their resources through collaborative projects with experienced Wikipedia editors.[6]

After the training session, Katie Filbert, a multitalented Wikimedia volunteer, came to the Archives of American Art for an in-person meeting. We explained our main goals in working with the online encyclopedia: First, we wanted researchers to find Archives of American Art content and linked citations on relevant Wikipedia pages and, when appropriate, to follow those links back to our website at aaa.si.edu. Second, we wanted to gain a better understanding of how Wikipedia works and to create relationships with the volunteer community.

Katie helped lay the groundwork for a more systematic project. Through her I started to gain an understanding of how Wikipedia works and absorbed the most important lesson about it: Wikipedia is only as good as the passion and drive of the volunteer community behind it. Fortunately for the world, they are an incredibly committed bunch.

In spring of 2011, Katie introduced me to Sarah Stierch, a museum studies master's student and prolific Wikipedia contributor. Sarah agreed to join the Archives of American Art as a summer intern and act as the Smithsonian Institution's first Wikipedian in residence—delivering a crash course in Wikipedian culture.[7]

IMPLEMENTATION

Through her own edits and activity, Sarah set an example of how to be a successful contributor on Wikipedia by not shying away from discussion or debate. She shook her head at the story of how we had allowed other editors to frighten us off with their accusation of spamming. She explained that, while there are guidelines we should try to follow, no single editor—even a very experienced one—has absolute power or authority over any other editor. This includes the administrator who decided to block the AAA intern account. On Wikipedia everything is open for debate! So, instead of backing down or running away when confronted, she explained that we should have stuck around and defended the value of our contributions.

While Sarah contributed to hundreds of Wikipedia articles during the months that she was with us, editing articles was not her focus. Her primary contributions consisted of training and teaching, content analysis, and outreach and events.

Her first and most important task was demystifying how Wikipedia works. This meant hands-on training for us in the technical aspects of the platform and being on site to answer questions when they occurred to us. Interested staff members queried her on the user interface, best practices, and community norms and culture. She presented a series of training workshops for Smithsonian staff from across the various museums and research centers, covering such topics as citing sources, conflict of interest, and media rights and usage.[8]

This training laid essential groundwork. Seemingly simple things can sometimes confound newcomers to Wikipedia; there is so much for a beginner to learn. For example, did you know you can search for information *about* Wikipedia—as opposed to the content of actual encyclopedia articles—by typing "Wikipedia:" (or the shortcut "WP:") into Wikipedia's search box? That new messages on talk pages always appear at the bottom and must be "signed" by entering four tildes? That contributors can earn awards or badges known as "barnstars"? I did not know any of these things when I first started, but I do now, thanks to having a helpful Wikipedian working a few seats away from me for several months.

The content analysis piece of Sarah's residency was also incredibly useful. We know that researchers at our archives are very name driven, as they are frequently looking for information on a specific artist. We wanted to know how many of our collection creators had Wikipedia biographies already so that we could make a plan for enhancing those biographies with content and links from the archives. We used our collections database to generate a CSV file consisting of individual creator names as well as their birth and death years. Stierch used her connections with some tech-savvy Wikimedia volunteers in Europe to automate the analysis of information exported from our collections database. The volunteers were able to run a script to compare the names and birth/death years against Wikipedia's data and to identify cases where the names were likely the same person. Relevant articles were then tagged with a Wikipedia project template on their talk pages, indicating that they are associated with a Wikipedia editing project at the Archives of American Art. The template includes a space for indicating the quality of the article per Wikipedia's assessment standards (e.g., Is it a very short stub or a medium-quality "C"?) as well as its importance to the archives' project. For example, we decided that artists whose papers we own and have digitized are of top importance, while those we have a short oral history interview with may just be of midlevel importance. Using a standard reporting tool hosted on Wikimedia Toolserver (now called Wikimedia Labs), the volunteers could leverage our project template data to create a report (see figure 7.1) showing us the names and URLs of 716 articles on Wikipedia about our collection creators. We have continually used this report to identify opportunities for improvements and new linkages. As we add new project templates to article talk pages, they are automatically incorporated into the report. We still use this report as the basis for editing projects today, seeking to improve the articles rated as top importance first.

Beyond providing training and assessment, Sarah also rallied the Wikimedia community to our cause. She allied us with the growing GLAM-Wiki initiative, which was starting to feature additional examples of Wikipedians in residence in the United States in places like the Children's Museum of Indianapolis and the National Archives and Records

Archives of American Art-related articles by quality and importance

Quality	Importance						
	Top	High	Mid	Low	NA	???	Total
⊕ GA	1						1
B	5	4	7	15			31
C	18	12	16	33			79
Start	42	66	52	170		1	331
Stub	40	47	38	148		1	274
List						2	2
NA					2		2
Assessed	106	129	113	366	2	4	720
Unassessed			1	1		1	3
Total	106	129	114	367	2	5	723
WikiWork factors (?)	$\omega = 3{,}710$				$\Omega = 5.18$		

Figure 7.1.   Archives of American Art-related Wikipedia biographies, ranked by quality and importance to the organization.

Administration. She tied our work to a global movement but also reached out personally to local Wikipedians and to any contributors who had demonstrated interest in articles relating to the visual arts in America. The result was a list of more than forty volunteers who signed up to participate—both virtually and in person—via our Archives of American Art project page.

I never expected that I would meet many of these Wikipedians in person, but Sarah announced that a "backstage pass tour and edit-a-thon" was a must-have event because it would give us the chance to get to know the community face to face. In August we planned a daylong event and invited around twenty of these volunteers to visit the archives in person. The schedule was to include a welcome address from our director, a tour, collections show-and-tell presentations from our archivists, lunch, and an afternoon of collaborative work using the archives' resources to improve a series of Wikipedia articles related to the 1913 Armory Show, an important art historical event about to celebrate its centennial. We were accustomed to having a handful of researchers at a time visiting our reading room, but very rarely had the doors of the archives ever been opened up to the public in such a way. As the event drew closer, I began to feel nervous. Would the Wikipedians respect and appreciate our work and our collections? Would the archivists and other staff accept the contributions of a group of "amateurs"?

The event ended up being one of the most inspirational days I have ever had at my job. Watching a multigenerational gathering of Wikipedians, staff, and interns working side by side in a room filled with laptops, I realized that the word *crowdsourcing* doesn't really capture the essence of people's contributions. There is no mere "crowd" on Wikipedia; rather, there is a vibrant community of intelligent, unique individuals with a variety of strengths and interests, united in their shared purpose to record and freely share the sum of the world's knowledge. At the edit-a-thon I had the privilege of meeting some of Wikipedia's most dedicated editors, seeing their faces, and learning the real names behind their online handles. Wikipedia editors could never be an undifferentiated mass to me again. The encyclopedia entries they have constructed bear the trace of their individualized contributions, recorded indefinitely on each article's "edit history" page.[9]

As a final project to commemorate the end of Sarah Stierch's residency, the archives decided to give back to the Wikipedia volunteer community by offering one of the things they prize most: a set of high-quality, high-resolution, public domain images uploaded to Wikimedia Commons. Wikimedia Commons is the media file repository that hosts all of the free images that you see illustrating Wikipedia articles. Typically, uploads to this site proceed slowly, one by one. However, Sarah worked with Katie Filbert to produce a script that facilitated the mass upload of more than three hundred public domain images from the archives to the

Wikimedia Commons accompanied by all of the specific metadata and backlinks that we requested. Each image also included a template, branded with our logo, acknowledging that the contribution was made as part of a cooperation project between the Archives of American Art and Wikipedia.[10]

RESULTS

Sarah continued her involvement with the Smithsonian, serving as Wikipedian in residence for the Smithsonian Institution Archives from March to June 2012. The biggest result of having a Wikipedian in residence for those months was a significantly higher internal expertise and interest in Wikipedia all across the Smithsonian. Smithsonian libraries, archives, and museums have now hosted a total of eleven public edit-a-thon events, with additional events being added to the calendar regularly in 2014. In June 2013, with support from the Office of the Secretary—the highest level of Smithsonian leadership—we were able to bring on our first pan-institutional Smithsonian Wikipedian in residence to help us continue the work of assessment, training, and strategizing for future collaboration.

Although the majority of the feedback that we have received from staff and from the public has been positive, not everybody was or is keen on collaborating with Wikipedia. An encyclopedia that anyone can edit is still viewed with suspicion by people who worry that it dismisses the importance of experts or disregards the authority of traditional reference works. Even the critics, however, tend to caveat their remarks with the admission that that they use it regularly!

As of July 2013, the Archives of American Art has 1,682 inbound links from 1,150 different Wikipedia pages.[11] Archives of American Art staff have added only a few hundred of them ourselves. For the last two years, these inbound links have steadily generated 5.25 percent of our total website traffic. This makes Wikipedia our single biggest referrer of inbound link traffic, more significant in terms of quantity than any social media site, Smithsonian website, or research catalog. Obviously, we would be pleased if the number of inbound referrals from Wikipedia increases over time, but that is not the only goal of our project. We know that there are many Wikipedia visitors who see our content on the encyclopedia but who don't click through on the reference link back to http://www.aaa.si.edu. And why should they? For more casual research, the information found on Wikipedia is probably sufficient to supply their answers. For a more intensive or scholarly inquiry, the archives' citation is at the ready in Wikipedia's footnotes for researchers who need to dig deeper.

For example, we can look at inbound traffic from Wikipedia to the Walt Kuhn papers.[12] Over a recent 90-day period, Wikipedia referrals to the Walt Kuhn finding aid account for 151 page views—7.2 percent of the 2,105 total page views for that particular finding aid. Compare that to the Walt Kuhn page on Wikipedia, which received 2,228 page views in the same time period. That means that only 6.8 percent of the Wikipedia article readers clicked through to our finding aid. However, more than two thousand others saw our name and our contributions to the article (image, citation, and external link) on the Walt Kuhn Wikipedia article, even though they didn't click through to our website.[13] By integrating our content into Walt Kuhn's biography on Wikipedia, we effectively doubled the exposure for the Archives of American Art's collections and knowledge relating to Walt Kuhn during that ninety-day period (from 2,105 page views on the archives' website alone, to 4,333 page views on both platforms).

Based on the most recent two years of web traffic data, we can make some general observations about visitors who reach our website via links from Wikipedia. Overall, they are:

- More self-sufficient—Wikipedia-referred visitors are significantly less likely to submit an inquiry to our "Ask Us" reference e-mail form than visitors who are referred by search engines (see figure 7.2).[14] Yet they seem similarly engaged with our website, viewing a nearly identical number of pages and spending an average of the same amount of time on site as search engine–referred visitors. They are a self-sufficient type of customer, one who ends up putting less of a burden on reference staff.
- More international—44 percent of Wikipedia-referred visits originate outside of the United States, with the vast majority of those coming from Western Europe. Compare this to 29.2 percent for all visits. In fact, although the majority of our Wikipedia visitors are referred by the English version of the encyclopedia, we also see noticeable traffic from the German, French, and Spanish Wikipedias, among other languages.
- Not just there for the pretty pictures—Based on analysis of the archives web directory structure, landing pages, and "content drill-down" behavior, it becomes clear that search engine–driven visitors are twice as likely as Wikipedia-referred visitors to be visiting the image gallery to see selected digital highlights from our collections. Wikipedia-referred visitors, by contrast, are more likely to be visiting oral history interviews, finding aids, and fully digitized collections. This makes sense, as they are typically following a textual citation from the encyclopedia, leading them to an interview or finding aid rather than an image.

When cultural institutions like the Archives of American Art partner with Wikipedia, we benefit from the collaboration, but so do our volunteers and so do the millions of readers of the encyclopedia. Other important (but less quantitatively measurable) examples of successful results relate directly to our relationships with our audiences, researchers, and donors.

Participating in Wikipedia opens up opportunities for outreach and creates educational opportunities for new audiences. One of the reasons Wikipedia editors enjoy contributing to the encyclopedia is because it is a learning activity. It provides a satisfying and fun intellectual challenge while also giving you the impression that you have made the world (or at least the web) a little bit better. Success measured in this light means that volunteers come away with a better understanding of our repository and the nature and value of archival resources in general and a better knowledge of the people and subjects that our collections document.

Our work with the Wikipedia community is also a catalyst to examine openness and understand the researcher experience. Each time we invite

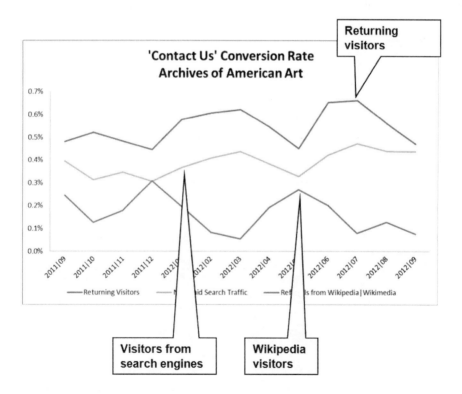

Figure 7.2.   Wikipedia-referred visitors tend to be self-serve customers. They are less likely to submit reference e-mails than visitors referred by search engines.

Wikipedians to work with us, they raise questions about our level of open access in the information and assets that we provide online. This often includes discussions around restrictions, copyright, and terms of use. Wikipedia and the Wikimedia Commons have extremely strict guidelines for image upload and sharing, and as a result the community tends to be fairly well versed in the laws that govern sharing and reuse.

The innocent questions raised by our Wikipedia volunteers frequently cut to the core of our discipline: "Why don't you have metadata for every single letter?" "What is a finding aid?" "Is oral history considered a primary or secondary source?" "When do you plan on digitizing the video?" These moments remind our staff (especially those of us who aren't on the front lines of reference work) how archives look from a user's perspective.

On occasion, encouraged by a request to use a particular image or read an interview transcript for the purpose of improving a Wikipedia article, we have gone back and reviewed the deed of gift or donor restrictions on a particular collection. At a recent edit-a-thon event, such a request actually led the registrar to call a ninety-year-old donor and ask her if it would be possible to lift the restriction on her oral history interview. Not only did the donor agree, but she also mentioned that she might have some additional material she would like to give to the archives. This interaction might never have happened without the catalyst of the edit-a-thon and the desire to reference the interview for a Wikipedia article.

We also appreciate the potential for increasing our social impact by increasing presence of underrepresented groups on Wikipedia. Our latest edit-a-thon at the Archives of American Art was not only about raising awareness of the contributions of women in the arts by improving a set of Wikipedia articles, but it was also about attempting to recruit more women to edit Wikipedia.[15] According to recent surveys, less than 15 percent of Wikipedia's regular contributors are women, and nobody can come to a reliable conclusion about why exactly that should be.[16] This statistic shocked me when I first read it. Surely the "sum of all human knowledge" couldn't be a story told almost entirely by men (again). This statistic motivated me to step up my outreach to librarians and archivists as Wikipedia contributors—not only does our professional training make us exceptionally well qualified to add reliable sources to Wikipedia articles, but we also tend to be a female-dominated profession.[17]

With so few women contributing, it is therefore not surprising that the encyclopedia is deficient in biographies of notable women and topics important to women. Intentionally or not, sexism is woven into the structure of many articles. The good news, however, is that Wikipedia can be edited by *anyone*. Therefore, women and other underrepresented groups have an unprecedented opportunity to join together and change this situation; in prior centuries a biased encyclopedia had no such remedy. We saw one example of a movement to address this problem in March 2013, when feminists organized "#TooFEW: the Feminist People of Color Wikipedia Edit-a-thon." [18]

President of the American Historical Association William Cronon has eloquently expressed Wikipedia's potential to rectify the traditional neglect of marginalized or niche histories:

> Perhaps most importantly, Wikipedia provides an online home for people interested in histories long marginalized by the traditional academy. The old boundary between antiquarianism and professional history collapses in an online universe where people who love a particular subject can compile and share endless historical resources for its study in ways never possible before. [19]

"Endless historical resources"? Sounds like archives to me!

One completely unexpected result of working on Wikipedia is the fact that, while editing the encyclopedia myself, I have bumped into donors and relatives of people whose papers we have in the archives. Perhaps I should have expected to see them online (Who else but her heirs should I expect to find tending the flame of Grandma's Wikipedia page?), but the first time it happened, I was taken aback. *What are* you *doing here?*

The donors and family members had noticed my edits on pages related to topics or people they care about, noted that I work for the Archives of American Art, and taken the time to introduce themselves on my user talk page. In one case I ended up helping to advise the relative on best practices and avoiding conflict of interest in an article about his great-grandfather, a noted American artist. He and I have a nice little online epistolary relationship now on our Wikipedia talk pages. Who knows who I will run into next—maybe someone with papers to donate?

LESSONS LEARNED

The Archives of American Art plans to continue strengthening our relationship with Wikipedia volunteers and to continue sharing our experience with our colleagues. We have absorbed several valuable lessons over the years about how cultural institutions can work effectively with the Wikipedia community.

First, every contribution we make must serve the goal of making the encyclopedia better. "Here to build an encyclopedia" is a long-standing mantra in the Wikipedia community. Today it serves as a kind of test to help us distinguish constructive and nonconstructive edits. If we violate this principle and add content that does not improve the encyclopedia, we could see our edits reverted and, worse, lose the good faith of the community. The best edits we can make include improvements to the body or images in the article, citing our finding aids, exhibitions, and publications as references.

We have also learned the importance of identifying the internal boosters on staff. In my experience there has to be at least one strong advocate on your staff to be a liaison to the community—though more than one is better! Unless you can hire a Wikipedian in residence permanently, somebody has to keep continuity in the relationship with the volunteers. I have yet to persuade a disinterested person to get involved; Wikipedia is just not everyone's cup of tea. Opening up the call for collaborators seems to work best, so that any Wikipedians on staff (be they aspiring or already active) can emerge from the woodwork. Where they sit in the organization is less important than the fact that they are open and interested in Wikipedia.

In addition, we have discovered that there is tremendous value in finding local Wikipedian mentors. The big turning point for the archives came when we first met up with very experienced Wikipedia contributors face to face. Aside from meeting people on Wikipedia itself, Meet-up.com groups, local Wikimedia chapters or clubs, Twitter, and e-mail lists have been great places to connect with Wikipedians (the GLAM-wiki listserv is a good place to ask for help or the names of local contacts: https://lists.wikimedia.org/mailman/listinfo/glam).

Finally, we have come to understand the powerful ties of shared culture that binds editors within the Wikipedia volunteer community. Wikipedia contributors span the globe, but they are surprisingly united in their sense of belonging to a singular, collective, open-knowledge movement. Their community values freedom and boldness; it also makes use of lots of insider acronyms and jargon. Overall, it comprises a culture unto itself that is unlike any other social media site.[20] We at the archives have had to learn how to view (and portray) ourselves on Wikipedia not as an institutional voice but as individual voices and contributors, no more inherently authoritative than the next.

CONCLUSION

The Archives of American Art, and the Smithsonian Institution more broadly, continue to enjoy an evolving and genial relationship of mutual benefit with our Wikipedia volunteers. After inviting them back into the archives again and again over the last few years, physically and virtually, they are no longer anonymous strangers. They have grown to understand our collections and have personal relationships with our staff, e-mailing or tweeting us with questions. Because all of their conversations happen in public—Wikipedia's discussion pages are viewable by anyone—they give us a clear glimpse into the thought process that researchers go through in making sense of our digital collections.

In addition to hosting more events and continuing to sponsor Wikipedians in residence, there are many opportunities still waiting to be explored. Our summer 2013 Wikipedian in residence, Dominic McDevitt-Parks, is already helping us to make progress on a number of these ideas. Some future projects include:

- Finding efficient workflows for integrating new information about our collections into Wikipedia and for assessing and reporting our success
- Creating new tools and templates to make it faster and easier for volunteer contributors to use and cite our resources on Wikipedia
- Promoting greater project organization by analyzing, optimizing, and documenting our "categories" (a system of tags) applied to articles and assets on Wikipedia and Wikimedia Commons
- Increasing technical competence among our staff on the Wikimedia platforms and MediaWiki API
- Sponsoring competitions or challenges to incentivize volunteers to improve an article and then nominate it as a "Did You Know?" or "Featured Article," both of which are displayed prominently on the home page of Wikipedia
- Reincorporating Wikipedia's open data back into our own projects or websites

The point I emphasize when talking to my fellow archivists, librarians, and museum professionals about Wikipedia is that, in the most basic sense, Wikipedians are just volunteers. Cultural heritage organizations like ours tend to have a great history of working with volunteers. The fact that their volunteerism occurs in the digital sphere does not change the fact that they are motivated by the same factors that motivate in-person volunteers: the desire to spend their free time intellectually engaged, to do something to make the world a little bit better, and to receive acknowledgment and appreciation for the contributions they have made. We should recruit these volunteers to work side by side with us, thank them for their hard work, and be respectful of the remarkable tool that they have built together over the last dozen years. Creating the world's largest free encyclopedia is an ambitious project but a worthy one, and more than ever its creators welcome contributions and collaboration from archives and archivists.

Sara Snyder is the webmaster at the Archives of American Art, Smithsonian Institution.

NOTES

1. Ann Lally, "Using Wikipedia to Highlight Digital Collections at the University of Washington," *The Interactive Archivist: Case Studies in Utilizing Web 2.0 to Improve the Archival Experience*, Society of American Archivists, May 18, 2009, http://interactivearchivist.archivists.org/case-studies/wikipedia-at-uw; Michael Szajewski,

"Using Wikipedia to Enhance the Visibility of Digitized Archival Assets," *D-Lib Magazine* 19, no. 3/4 (March/April 2013), accessed April 10, 2013, http://www.dlib.org/dlib/march13/szajewski/03szajewski.html .

2. For a helpful account of the debate that was taking place within the Wikipedia community at that time, see Michele Combs, "Wikipedia as an Access Point for Manuscript Collections," in *A Different Kind of Web: New Connections between Archives and Our Users*, ed. Kate Theimer (Chicago: Society of American Archivists, 2011), 139–47.

3. "User Talk: Aaa Intern," *Wikipedia*, accessed April 2, 2013, https://en.wikipedia.org/wiki/User_talk:Aaa_intern.

4. Noam Cohen, "Venerable British Museum Enlists in the Wikipedia Revolution," *New York Times*, June 4, 2010, http://www.nytimes.com/2010/06/05/a rts/design/05wiki.html.

5. For a full account of that meeting and the history of the Smithsonian's collaboration with Wikipedia, see the project page "Wikipedia: GLAM/Smithsonian Institution," *Wikipedia*, accessed July 2, 2013, https://en.wikipedia.org/wiki/Wikipedia:GLAM/SI.

6. For an ongoing list of libraries, museums, and archives that have formally collaborated with the Wikimedia community, see "Wikipedia: GLAM/Projects" at https://en.wikipedia.org/wiki/Wikipedia:GLAM/Projects.

7. Sarah Stierch, "A Very Wiki Summer: First Wikipedian-in-Residence for the Smithsonian Institution to Join the Archives of American Art in June," *Archives of American Art Blog*, May 4, 2011, http://blog.aaa.si.edu/2011/05/first-smithsonian-wikipedian-in-residence-at-the-archives-of-american-art.html.

8. A list of Stierch's talks can be found at "Wikipedia: GLAM/Archives of American Art/Brown Bags" at https://en.wikipedia.org/wiki/Wikipedia:GLAM/Archives_of_American_Art/Brown_bags.

9. The first "backstage pass and edit-a-thon" at the Archives of American Art was covered by a journalist the *Chronicle of Philanthropy*. You can see some of the participants interviewed in a video that he produced for the occasion at "How the Smithsonian Is Helping Wikipedia" at http://philanthropy.com/blogs/social-philanthropy/how-the-smithsonian-is-helping-wikipedia/29095.

10. For a summary of all of the activities that comprised the archives' Wikipedian-in-residency, see "Wikipedia: GLAM/Archives of American Art" at https://en.wikipedia.org/wiki/Wikipedia:GLAM/AAA.

11. Ed Summers, "Featured Website: Archives of American Art, Smithsonian Institution." *Linkypedia*, accessed July 18, 2013, http://linkypedia.info/websites/54.

12. "A Finding Aid to the Walt Kuhn, Kuhn Family Papers, and Armory Show records, 1859–1978, Bulk 1900–1949," *Archives of American Art*, accessed April 20, 2013, http://www.aaa.si.edu/collections/walt-kuhn-kuhn-family-papers-and-armory-show-records-9172/more.

13. Data on Wikipedia page views of Walt Kuhn from January to March 2013 comes from http://stats.grok.se/en/latest30/Walt%20Kuhn.

14. Credit for this analysis goes to Brian Alpert, who manages web and social media analytics for the Smithsonian Institution. For more detail see his presentation, "Click Here for Customized Data: Google Analytics Automated Dashboard" (Museums and the Web, Portland, OR, April 2013).

15. "Wikipedia: Meetup/DC/Women in the Arts 2013," *Wikipedia*, March 29, 2013, accessed April 20, 2013, http://en.wikipedia.org/wiki/Wikipedia:Meetup/DC/Women_in_the_Arts2013.

16. "Where Are the Women in Wikipedia?" *New York Times*, February 2, 2011, http://www.nytimes.com/roomfordebate/2011/02/02/where-are-the-women-in-wikipedia.

17. I expanded on this idea in a guest blog post, "Bring on the Chicks with Glasses!: Why Wiki Loves Libraries and GLAM-Wiki Can Help Address the Wikipedia Gender Gap," *Wikimedia Foundation*, November 12, 2012, http://blog.wikimedia.org/2012/11/12/bring-on-the-chicks-with-glasses-why-wiki-loves-libraries-glam-wiki-can-help-address-the-wikipedia-gender-gap.

18. Adeline Koh, "#TooFEW: Feminist People of Color Wikipedia Edit-a-Thon on Friday, March 15 (2013) from 11 a.m.–3 p.m. EST," *The Chronicle of Higher Education*, March 12, 2013, https://chronicle.com/blogs/profhacker/toofew-feminist-people-of-color-wikipedia-edit-a-thon-on-friday-11am-3pm-est/47265.

19. William Cronon, "Scholarly Authority in a Wikified World," *Perspectives on History*, February 2012, http://www.historians.org/perspectives/issues/2012/1202/Scholarly-Authority-in-a-Wikified-World.cfm.

20. For an interesting profile of the average Wikipedia contributor, see Sue Gardner, "Wikipedia, the People's Encyclopedia," *Los Angeles Times*, January 13, 2013, http://articles.latimes.com/2013/jan/13/opinion/la-oe-gardner-wikipedia-20130113.

EIGHT

21 Revolutions

New Art from Old Objects

Laura Stevens, Glasgow Women's Library

Glasgow Women's Library (GWL) opened its doors in Garnethill, Glasgow, in 1991. GWL represented a more permanent evolution of the broad-based arts organization Women in Profile (WIP), which was launched in 1987 to ensure that the representation of women's culture was visible during the city's tenure as the European City of Culture in 1990. GWL remains an important legacy for the city from that year.

Glasgow Women's Library is unique in Scotland and has developed into the key hub for information on gender and women. GWL's collection, comprised of a lending library, archive, and museum, houses a significant range of feminist- and women's issues–related material represented at local, national, and international levels. It has a collection of materials that link the suffragette campaigns of the nineteenth and early twentieth centuries to the explosion of political campaigns and social shifts brought about by second-wave feminist activism from the 1970s onward. Items in the GWL's collections are wide ranging, encompassing texts, posters, badges, banners, pamphlets, and materials that relate to the diverse array of women's lives and experiences, from radical feminist literature to lesbian "dime" novels, dressmaking patterns to recipe books.

Begun in September 2011 and launched at GWL's twentieth-anniversary celebrations, the project "21 Revolutions: Two Decades of Changing Minds at Glasgow Women's Library" was the culmination of a year's work celebrating GWL's twenty-first birthday. To demonstrate the continuum between the past and present, GWL commissioned twenty-one of

Scotland's most renowned women artists and twenty-one women writers to each create new works inspired by items in the library, archive, and museum collections. The artists each created limited-edition fine art prints, and the writers produced short stories or poems. These exclusively commissioned prints were then available for purchase to support GWL's ongoing work, while the writers' works were recorded by them and released by GWL in a series of free downloadable podcasts.[1]

The new works draw on sources including campaign badges, knitting patterns, suffragette memorabilia, album covers, recipe books, feminist newsletters, and a myriad of books from the GWL shelves. The project provided an excellent opportunity to showcase the resources in GWL's collections, highlighting the materials in our care to new audiences, as well as raising the organization's profile and generating income.

The "21 Revolutions" project was conceived and managed by GWL's senior management team: Adele Patrick, lifelong learning and creative development manager, and Sue John, enterprise development manager, and supported by volunteer and participating artist Helen de Main. Both Sue and Adele studied at Glasgow School of Art, and Adele also taught there for several years. When funding was secured for the project, Helen became a paid exhibition cocurator.

The collections team, consisting of the librarian and the archivist, were also crucial to the success of the project. Prior to 2009 GWL's archive was under the care of volunteers working within the library. In 2009 GWL submitted a successful funding bid to the Heritage Lottery Fund for capital to build a dedicated Women's Archive of Scotland and for a three-year project to employ a professional archivist. Hannah Little was appointed as GWL's first archivist in September 2009 and was active in the planning stages of the "21 Revolutions" project. In September 2010, I was appointed to provide maternity cover for Hannah. The collections team during the "21 Revolutions" project comprised the GWL archivist (both Hannah and I) and the librarian, Wendy Kirk, supported by a team of volunteers. Since its foundation volunteers have played an integral role in GWL's development, and they were invaluable to the "21 Revolutions" project.

PLANNING

As GWL's twenty-first anniversary approached, our senior management team was keen to mark this important milestone. The planning stage began in early 2011. Drawing on the strong support and links developed over twenty-one years between the GWL and both the visual arts and writers' communities as well as their connections with Glasgow's art community, we soon developed ideas on how the celebration could involve these creative collaborators. Keeping with the "twenty-one" theme, it was decided to recruit twenty-one women respectively from the artistic and writing fields, and the senior management team, supported by Helen, devised their "wish list" of people they would like to approach. After the initial planning stages had been carried out, it was time to pursue funding for what become known as the "21 Revolutions" project.

A successful funding application was submitted to both Museums Galleries Scotland and Creative Scotland, with confirmation received on October 7, 2011, and January 20, 2012, respectively. While the senior management team was awaiting confirmation of the funding, they continued with the planning stages. The collections team selected a sample of sources as a start to inspire the project participants. This was challenging, especially as two thirds of the collection was in external storage with limited access and the team had a wide range of materials from which to choose. The library's lending collection is an extensive resource, containing a variety of books ranging from fiction written by women to niche monograph works, which users can borrow using their membership cards. The archive is also home to the United Kingdom's National Lesbian Archive as well as GWL's institutional records and many deposited collections from across Scotland. GWL's museum contains a collection of artifacts ranging from a Victorian umbrella stand painted in the campaign colors of purple, green, and white by suffragettes incarcerated in Duke Street Prison to badges, T-shirts, posters, and other ephemera.

A finding aid showcasing the sample material selected from each area by the collections team was tailor-made for the project participants. Wendy selected a wide sample of texts from the lending collection that ranged from seminal feminist set texts, such as *The Female Eunuch* by Germaine Greer; books by women artists, including Georgia O'Keefe; and texts focusing on women's history, such as *Grit and Diamonds: Women in Scotland Making History 1980–1990*. Meanwhile, Hannah selected materials from the archive that capitalized on the strengths within the collection, such as the suffragette collection, journals collection, and such ephemera as knitting and dressmaking patterns. These were intended to inspire the participants, and they were welcome to explore other areas within the collection.

The senior management team also had to decide what direction and products they wanted as results for the project. After discussions it was decided that the artists would be requested to produce a print edition of up to twenty, with one copy of each print kept for GWL's archive, while the remaining works would be sold to raise funds for GWL. For the writers a similar request was made by asking them to produce a new piece of work of up to 1,500 words. The project brief was made flexible to allow participants to have a degree of creative freedom in keeping with the style of their work.

The team also needed to select the participants who would be inspired by the materials we had selected. A list of women was gathered together, drawing on the library's own pool of contacts in the Scottish creative sphere. Adele and Sue convened selection meetings with GWL colleague Donna Moore (a published writer), member of the GWL board of directors; Zoe Strachan (also a published writer); Helen De Main (printmaker); and Claire Barclay (an established artist with an international profile and past member of Women in Profile). This selection team aimed to ensure that artists and writers ranged from established, well-known practitioners to emerging talent, as well as women who were familiar with GWL's history and collections and those who were new to our work. The team was keen to involve women who worked in distinct ways and different disciplines, from lithographers to screen printers and indeed those new to printmaking. A list of practitioners to approach was researched and compiled. Contact was made with these women, and fortunately for the project, everyone who was able and available said they were delighted to take part due to their existing knowledge and support of GWL and its work. The main points of contact during this process were Adele and Sue. During the exhibition preparation stages of the project, Helen also played a key role in keeping contact with the participants, with support from volunteers.

With our participants confirmed, the artists and writers were commissioned with a small one-time fee to be paid to each made possible by the support of Creative Scotland and Museums Galleries Scotland. Some were emerging talents in their field, such as artist Delphine Dallison and writer Kirsty Logan, while others were internationally renowned, established names, including two Turner Prize nominees (Karla Black and Lucy Skaer) and Scotland representatives at the Venice Biennale (Claire Barclay and Corin Sworn), along with writers A. L. Kennedy, Jackie Kay, and Louise Welsh. The funds provided by Creative Scotland also allowed GWL to pay for the artworks to be framed. Additionally, this fund was used to print such promotional materials as postcards and invitations.

The collections team knew that the experience levels with handling archival material ranged widely among the project participants. Some women had worked with GWL's collection before, while for others this was the first time they visited the library. It was agreed that each participant would have a one-on-one introductory session with a member of the collections team. This would allow the participants to tap into the collections knowledge held by the team as well as introduce them to the basics of archival search-room practices.

Spreadsheets emerged as the best method of capturing information vital to the project. The collections team set up a dedicated spreadsheet to capture key data relating to the participants' time in the library that recorded information, including which material they consulted on their visits, any follow-up research that was required, and any indications of when their return visits might be.

During the planning stages, it was decided to stagger the project submission deadlines for the participants. The first deadline was in March 2012, with the second deadline in June 2012. These staggered deadlines were a great assistance to the collections team. It allowed us to manage project participants accessing the collection alongside other researchers.

IMPLEMENTATION

A welcoming and networking event for the project participants took place in January 2012 at the library. Adele was keen to provide networking opportunities for the individuals participating in the project. At this stage we did not know whether participants would choose to collaborate with one another, but we wanted to give them a chance to meet with each other to discuss their work to see if any collaborations might emerge. The meeting was also an opportunity to pass on generic information and answer questions as well as to introduce people to samples from the collection. This allowed the artists and writers to mingle together and share ideas about the project so far. It also allowed for artists and writers that were well established in their careers to meet with women who were emerging talents in their field.

Each participant was invited to an individual orientation session with a member of the collections team, with the sessions beginning in September 2011 shortly after the launch event. At this session we introduced the participants to the rest of the team and gave them a copy of the finding aid for the materials we had selected as a "starter" set for the project. The participants were also given the opportunity to discuss their initial ideas with the collections team in addition to an introduction to archive handling and our "housekeeping" guidelines. It was incredibly inspirational seeing these women accessing the material in the archive. One artist, Ashley Cook, spent hours closely examining a suffragette card game called "Panko!, and the influence can be clearly seen in her final artwork.[2] Kirsty Logan, one of the writers recruited onto the project, bridged the gap between art and writing by creating a story comprised of words photocopied from 1950s *Vogue* articles and other sources of "domestic" women's literature. Her original inspiration came from a record sleeve design from GWL's archive (see textbox 8.1)

Many of the project participants lived relatively close to the library, which made it easier for them to access the archival material. However, there were some individuals who were unable to physically come into GWL to access material from the collection. Two of the writers, A. L. Kennedy and Jackie Kay, could not come into GWL due to work commitments, so the collections team worked together to solve this problem. A member of the team established e-mail contact with both writers to determine the areas of the collection that each writer was interested in. Each

"I saw the cover of Lung Leg's album *Maid to Minx*, featuring a badass lady wrestler in a skull-and-crossbones cape, and I remembered Graham Rawle's book *Woman's World*, a novel made entirely from cut-out words. Why write a regular short story, I thought, when I could use this chance to do something a bit different? I decided to "write" a story about a female prizefighter from cut-out words: somewhere between fiction and visual art.

I spent a joyful few days immersed in GWL's archives, photocopying pages from various 1950s artifacts: women's fashion magazines, girls' annuals and traditional Scottish recipe books.

Next I cut out many, many words, got bored halfway through organising them into categories, and jumped right into trying to make a story. After a few days of this I found my point of despair, lying down among those 64 sheets of paper.

My girlfriend found me among the photocopies and told me, essentially, to get a bloody grip on myself (everybody needs someone in their life who will tell them such things). So I did. As soon as I started sticking the words down it all came together, and I was finished the next day. The final product was four sheets of A4, made entirely of 1950s magazines, telling the story of a female fighter. And I'm really, really proud of it."

Textbox 8.1. Kirsty Logan, writing about the origins of her original work, "This is Liberty"

writer was sent a copy of the inspiration sources that was initially given to each participant on their first visits to GWL. A. L. Kennedy specifically indicated that she would like to work with GWL's collection of knitting and dressmaking patterns. Samples from this collection were scanned and sent to her, using Dropbox to share the image files. Meanwhile, Jackie Kay proposed themes she would like to explore, such as ethnicity, identity, and representations of women. Using my knowledge of the collection, I followed a similar process by scanning in a taster of material and sending it to Jackie using Dropbox.

Jackie did find time to come into GWL to browse the collection toward the end of her deadline for the project in March 2013. On her visit I produced material from the papers of Ingrid McClements, who, unbeknown to me, had been an acquaintance of Jackie's before her death in 2008. Jackie was obviously moved by finding a link to her old friend in GWL's collection, and this provided inspiration for one of two poems that she produced for the project.

Some of the project participants requested help with additional research. This task was handed on to volunteers who had indicated they would like to be involved with the "21 Revolutions" project. One artist, Nicky Bird, had previously worked with the library on another project and had been supported by one of our volunteers, Alice Andrews. Fortunately this volunteer was still involved with the library and so was able to assist Nicky with the additional research required for her project. Nicky was working with a collection from the Lesbian Archive, a series of newsletters called the *Raging Dykes Network*. She was fascinated by the widespread geographic locations of network members and the large volumes of correspondence generated by the group. Alice was tasked with looking through the correspondence and pinpointing the locations of women involved with the network. Nicky's ideas were captured in a series of postcards representing the locations of the women belong to the *Raging Dykes Network*.[3]

While some artists were drawn to our sample list of inspirational materials, others became interested in more abstract elements of GWL. One artist, Ruth Barker, was keen to capture the atmosphere of the library and how users encountered the space. The collections team supported Ruth as much as we could by supplementing her work with access to the lending library, archive, and museum collections. Ruth's artwork ultimately focused on one of the most mundane ways researchers interact with the archive itself, taking the form of a digital print of a silk chiffon scarf:

> The central panel of each scarf shows an image of the artist's hands, in an aesthetic suggesting the humble photocopy. Part of the beauty and strength of the Library's archive are the sheaves of photocopied notes and advertisements, revealing the historical significance of this simple tool for sharing information.
>
> The Library is a quiet space, and yet through our body language— particularly the way we use our hands—we are always eloquent. The immensely warm and welcoming embrace of the Library and its community is celebrated in the scarves' enveloping wrap.[4]

RESULTS

Two public events took place at GWL in March and June 2012, where several writers launched their new works with readings against a backdrop of new artworks on display. The events drew full-capacity audiences of eighty people, many visiting the library for the first time. The culmination of the "21 Revolutions" project took place in September to October 2012 at the Centre for Contemporary Arts (CCA) in Glasgow, where all the artworks were exhibited together for the first time (see figure 8.1). The artists' inspiration sources from the collection were displayed to offer context to their finished work, as well as showing the richness of GWL's collection. Alongside the exhibition, the "21 Revolutions" team organized a complementary program of readings and gallery tours. The web manager at GWL was tasked with sampling all the artworks and uploading portrait photos of all the participants onto a new web page created for "21 Revolutions."[5]

GWL was fortunate to receive a range of press coverage, including a highlighted mention in *The List*,[6] a monthly events listings magazine covering events across Scotland. The *Scotland on Sunday*, a popular Sunday broadsheet distributed throughout the country, ran a two-page article in their weekend magazine a week prior to the launch of the exhibition, which included warm testimonials about the value of GWL from many of the "21 Revolutions" participants, including this one from Claire Barclay:

> The artist, who has represented Scotland at the Venice Biennale, was part of Women in Profile, the organisation that helped found GWL. "In the Eighties it was really important, because there was a sense that women's voices were not being heard. It was a support for young women artists. . . . These days, for me, it's about reconnecting with the library. The archives are incredible, but for me it's not just a conventional library resource, but a place of connection with other artists and writers."[7]

And this one from Muriel Gray:

Figure 8.1. At the exhibition launch, two of our Women's History tour guides and long-term users of GWL admiring the work of Sam Ainsley, who is credited with kick starting Glasgow's art scene in the 1980s (when the city was in a rapid decline due to the closure of its numerous shipyards).

> The writer and broadcaster . . . has written an essay inspired by the library's archive of marriage guidance literature. "GWL has always been an absolute oasis in the city, providing not just literary archive, information and entertainment, but also outreach, inspiration and positive messages for women of all backgrounds."[8]

An article also ran in *The Herald*, another popular Scottish broadsheet newspaper, promoting the "21 Revolutions" project, and again the project's participants spoke about how highly they valued the library and the opportunity to contribute to its future:

> Becoming a part of the women's library archive was one of the reasons that writer Laura Marney, whose own submission is a short story set in the Democratic Republic of Congo, wanted to be involved. "I feel it's an absolute privilege. It's the idea that you become part of women's artistic history in Glasgow. It's an honour."[9]

Adele and several writers were also featured on two Book Café programs on BBC Radio Scotland.[10]

The original writers' texts were donated to the collection, and the accompanying inspiring objects were exhibited together with them at GWL. This exhibition ran in tandem with the artists' exhibition taking place at the CCA. These works are the subject of series of monthly podcasts featuring each writer reading her own work and contextualizing it with descriptions of the sources of inspiration from the GWL archive collections. Adele recruited a sessional worker to liaise with each writer and schedule an interview in which they discussed the inspiration for their new works before reading the works themselves. These recordings were then edited and are uploaded to iTunes and the GWL website each month.[11] Fortunately a member of the library's staff already had experience in creating podcasts for the institution's series of Women's Heritage Walks, so the "21 Revolutions" team could call upon her existing skills and knowledge.

An additional exhibition was displayed at GWL alongside the writers' exhibition: "Revolution on Roller Skates." This captured the work of "21 Revolutions" contributor Ellie Harrison, founder of the National Museum of Roller Derby, now housed in GWL. Ellie combined her discovery of the feminist texts within GWL's lending library with her induction into the Glasgow Roller Derby League.

The "21 Revolutions" project substantially increased awareness of GWL and the importance of collecting items relating to women's lives, history, and achievements. It significantly raised the public profile of our work and issues around women and gender in the arts and heritage sectors. It enhanced GWL's reputation as an organization capable of staging and managing arts events and generated a cohort of forty-two artists and writers, including some of the most significant makers in Scotland, all of whom we now regard as supporters of our work. More than five hundred people attended the launch event of "21 Revolutions" at the Centre for Contemporary Arts—the most that the gallery had ever seen at an opening event. Approximately 2,200 people attended the exhibition and related public events in three weeks. These visitors included a range of users, including visitors from a local women's aid shelter, students from the Glasgow School of Art, members of the Glasgow Roller Derby league, and Glasgow-based art enthusiasts.

As noted, we have also succeeded in bring the work of the "21 Revolutions" artists and writers to people who could not visit the exhibitions. As of August 15, 2013, more than 1,900 unique visitors have accessed the project's webpages on the GWL website. Meanwhile, the monthly podcast series has received more than 1,100 unique downloads, bringing GWL's work and collections to a wider audience.

The project has also had a positive impact on GWL's ability to self-generate income, contributing to our aim to become less reliant on public funding. Copies from the limited editions of all fine art prints created are available to purchase, and the sales have been extremely positive, with more than £20,000 raised to date and all proceeds going back to support GWL's work. Prints have also been purchased by public collections, such as Glasgow's Gallery of Modern Art and the Royal Society of the Arts based in Edinburgh so that the works will be available to the public in the longer term. Seven of the artists' works have been reproduced as merchandise by GWL as bookmarks and postcards, available at GWL and via GWL's website. Another artwork, "Give a Damn: Advice Giver," has been reproduced on postcards to publicize GWL's other fund-raising activities, such as or becoming a "friend" of GWL or sponsoring a shelf under our "Women on the Shelf" scheme to raise capital funds for renovations to our new location.

LESSONS LEARNED

The "21 Revolutions" project was on a scale unlike any the library had attempted before. Inspiring, facilitating, and creating an exhibition showcasing the work of twenty-one artists and twenty-one writers was a remarkable feat for GWL. Our work supporting it required a learning curve for me and the rest of the collections team involved with working on the project.

One wise decision made by our management team was that the initial wish list of participants included more than forty-two artists and writers to allow for any women who would be unable to commit to the project. One of the artists approached to take part had to drop out in the early stages due to family obligations. This problem was easily addressed due to the existing long list, and another artist was approached and invited to participate. If your project relies on a set number, such as twenty-one artists and twenty-one writers to celebrate a twenty-first anniversary, it is a good idea to create a long list that exceeds your required quota.

GWL is fortunate to have a well-established network that allowed the senior management team to get assistance in identifying and approaching a variety of artists and writers to take part in the project. If you are considering a project of this kind, explore your own networks for recommendations of creative individuals. Alternatively, ask your local colleges or universities that run arts programs for their advice. A well-penned and polite e-mail outlining the project is a good way to make initial contact, especially if you do not know the potential participants you are approaching.

Following on from that, it was vital to keep communication between the collections team and project participants flowing. This helped us keep track of the direction in which the participants' work was going and whether it seemed to meet the objectives of the project. Making sure we communicated regularly was also a good way to ensure that the participants were getting the relevant support from the collections team and access to research material. As discussed earlier, some participants could not come into GWL. In these instances we worked with them to identify what materials appeared to be most relevant to their work, made digital copies of the material, and sent them to the participants via Dropbox. All of this interaction allowed us to build up relationships that were also helpful when it was time to remind participants of project deadlines.

There were three mixer events held at GWL to allow the artists and writers to meet and discuss their work. The mixer in January 2012 was a private event for the project participants, while the later mixer events, in March and June, were open to the public and also acted as a platform for the writers to perform their finished pieces of work. If you are planning a similar project, I recommend scheduling time for similar events. These mixers were wonderful opportunities for women with established careers to meet with emerging talents. They also allowed us to touch base with the project participants in an informal environment and away from the search room. Events that are open to the public can act as teasers for other events in the program, such as a large-scale exhibition, as was the case with "21 Revolutions."

For a small organization such as ours, we found it was vital to utilize other people as much as we could. Managing forty-two visitors to the archive, some for multiple visits, became a huge task for the collections team, especially as the librarian and I both work only part time. To alleviate this, volunteers were recruited to assist with such tasks as retrieving archival objects for the participants, carrying out any additional research, and administrative tasks, such as keeping our records of participants' inspirational source selections up to date. If our resources had permitted, I think it would have worked best to assign one member of the team to solely work on this project, especially in the initial stages when partici-pants are visiting the institution for the first time.

CONCLUSION

Activities relating to the "21 Revolutions" project continue on past the twenty-first anniversary year. The "21 Revolutions" exhibition was spe-cially selected to be showcased at the Creative Scotland Awards ceremo-ny and dinner, with four hundred people in attendance, on December 13, 2012. Another showcase of the exhibition was displayed at a popular Glasgow café and bar, Café Gandolfi, in March 2013 and received a popu-lar response. Significantly, due to its success and high caliber of artists involved, "21 Revolutions" was also exhibited at the Royal Scottish Acad-emy in Edinburgh during the Edinburgh Festival (July to September 2013), with several of the writers reading the works during the Edin-burgh Literary Festival Fringe in 2013.

A successful funding application has been submitted to Creative Scot-land to create a publication that will showcase the writers' and artists' contributions to "21 Revolutions." Three new essays will be commis-sioned, and the items from the collection that inspired the work will also be included.

The "21 Revolutions" project was successful in drawing attention to our twenty-first anniversary and opening up the collections to new audi-ences, encouraging them to see the items in a different light through the mediums of visual art and writing. This has been particularly important to us, as it comes at a time when GWL is relocating to a new building and urgently needs to raise funds for this purpose. The funds raised by the "21 Revolutions" project are a key factor in this relocation, but the fund-raising aspect of the project could be adapted for any archive wishing to pursue a new venture. However, the most important benefit for GWL of the project has been increasing our connections with our core constitu-ents—women across Scotland—and promoting the value of the past and future of documenting and studying their lives. The "21 Revolutions" project has allowed us to show new generations of women the value of the contributions of the women who came before them and so helped propel us forward into our next twenty-one years.

Laura Stevens is the archivist of the Glasgow Women's Library.

NOTES

1. For more information on the project, see "Two Decades of Changing Minds," *Glasgow Women's Library*, accessed October 25, 2013, http://womenslibrary.org.uk/about-us/our-history/two-decades-of-changing-minds.

2. "We Want: Exclusive Ltd Edition Digital Print and Screenprint by Ashley Cook," *Glasgow Women's Library*, accessed October 25, 2013, http://womenslibrary.org.uk/products-page/prints/we-want-print-by-ashley-cook.

3. "Raging Dyke Network: Exclusive Ltd Edition Colour Postcards by Nicky Bird with Alice Andrews," *Glasgow Women's Library*, accessed October 25, 2013, http://womenslibrary.org.uk/products-page/prints/raging-dyke-network-postcards-by-nicky-bird.

4. "A Scarf for Glasgow Women's Library: Exclusive Ltd Edition Digital Print on Silk by Ruth Barker," *Glasgow Women's Library*, accessed October 25, 2013, http://womenslibrary.org.uk/products-page/prints/a-scarf-for-gwl-print-on-silk-by-ruth-barker.

5. "21 Revolutions: The Artists," *Glasgow Women's Library*, accessed October 25, 2013, http://womenslibrary.org.uk/about-us/our-history/two-decades-of-changing-minds/21-revolutions-the-artists.

6. Talitha Kotze, "Glasgow Women's Library Hosts Group Exhibition 21 Revolutions," *The List*, September 7, 2012, http://www.list.co.uk/article/45243-glasgow-womens-library-hosts-group-exhibition-21-revolutions.

7. Moira Jeffrey, "A Host of Grateful Writers and Artists Will Help the Women's Library to Celebrate Its 20th Birthday," *The Scotsman*, September 9, 2012, http://www.scotsman.com/lifestyle/a-host-of-grateful-writers-and-artists-will-help-the-women-s-library-to-celebrate-its-20th-birthday-1-2514841.

8. Ibid.

9. Elizabeth McMeekin, "A Revolutionary Coming of Age," *The Herald*, September 13, 2012, http://www.heraldscotland.com/arts-ents/visual/a-revolutionary-coming-of-age.1347501856.

10. "The Book Café," *BBC Radio Scotland*, aired on September 24, 2012, and March 11, 2013.

11. "21 Revolutions Podcast," *Glasgow Women's Library*, accessed October 25, 2013, http://womenslibrary.org.uk/category/21-revolutions-podcast.

NINE

Happy Accidents and Unintended Consequences

How We Named Our Tribble

Rachael Dreyer, American Heritage Center

The American Heritage Center (AHC) at the University of Wyoming has engaged in social media through a blog, as well as Facebook and Twitter pages, since August 2010. Since its inception the media strategy that the AHC has employed has attempted to garner additional interest in our collections and services and has been informed by its internal 2010 Web 2.0 Task Force report.[1] Originally, caution informed the type of content that was disseminated through social media channels, so we limited ourselves to sharing things like announcements about newly processed collections, events, and lectures taking place at the AHC. However, as our comfort level has increased, we have shifted the structure of our social media outreach efforts from a broadcast device to an engagement tool. We now ask questions, request feedback, and field research questions through our Facebook, blog, and Twitter pages. This has had the effect of increasing the number of users who comment and otherwise actively respond to the messages that we convey.

Engaging users has been a goal for our online outreach from the beginning; our successes and ongoing challenges have shaped our evolving strategies. Our most successful online engagement activity to date has been our "Name the Tribble" contest, facilitated for American Archives Month in 2012. The contest allowed for interaction and engagement with a wide variety of potential users, enabled us to promote our collections and services to new audiences, and raised the AHC's online profile. This experience also provided us with a learning opportunity to look more closely at our online audience, evaluate our outreach strategies in the realm of social media, and gain a more concrete sense of what might be effective in future outreach efforts.

PLANNING

The "Name the Tribble" contest was not the AHC's first foray into a targeted social media strategy. In September 2012 the AHC attempted an activity that we called "Trivia Tuesday." Each Tuesday in September, we posted to Facebook and Twitter a trivia question related to Wyoming history or to our collections. Answers could be discovered by searching our collections or, in the case of the more general Wyoming history questions, with common knowledge. No prizes were awarded, and it was a low-intensity effort on our part. It received a correspondingly low level of participation, usually from among a relatively small group of "regulars." One possible explanation is that, once the question was answered by a member of our online audience, there was no incentive to contribute another answer. This social media flop indicated that we needed to encourage a wider range of participation, as our current efforts were reaching our "repeat customers." We also suspected that our efforts needed to incorporate greater incentives to participate.

While the "Trivia Tuesday" effort was not successful, it enabled us to better understand our existing community of online users, as well as to continue to improve our online outreach strategy. It was this quasi-failure that led in part to the success of the "Name the Tribble" contest. In designing the tribble contest, it was evident that, while there is intense interest in Wyoming history among our existing social media followers, many of these aficionados were already aware of the services and collections offered to the public. In order to reach the truly new audience we hoped, we needed to format our outreach effort for general appeal. In formulating our next campaign, we devised an incentivized contest to encourage participation from those who might otherwise not be inclined to take part, and we turned to one of our most popular and durable artifacts as the vehicle for the outreach activity—an original *Star Trek* tribble housed in the Forrest J. Ackerman papers.

Historically, the American Heritage Center had conducted extensive programming for Archives Week held in the fall of each year.[2] Archives Week at the AHC had usually involved a full schedule of activities for the entire week, often two public programs each day. Both outside lecturers and AHC archivists presented on topics that pertained to the AHC's holdings, such as the Wyoming Hereford Ranch, Carl Stalling's musical compositions, and local history. Programs also included film screenings as well as repository tours and off-site tours, such as a community walking tour highlighting local stained-glass windows and a Wyoming Hereford Ranch tour. While the aim was to engage and interact with users who might not ordinarily visit the archives, it became clear in discussions with senior AHC archivists that these programs attracted the same audiences each year. These programs required large investments of staff time to organize, facilitate, and, in many cases, present. According to long-time staff, other responsibilities, in addition to a certain level of burnout, contributed to the phasing out of these activities by the late 2000s.

As archives awareness campaigns became a more frequent activity for regional and national professional organizations, the AHC continued to participate in these regional outreach activities for Archives Month. However, AHC involvement included less in-depth participation, such as designing and hanging commemorative posters, rather than the more in-depth activities we'd sponsored with the earlier Archives Week activities. The most recent year in which the AHC participated in Archives Month activities was 2010, although even then the participation was limited. Involvement was channeled through the Society of Rocky Mountain Archivists; the AHC's contribution consisted of one of our archivists serving as Archives Month and outreach coordinator for the Society of Rocky Mountain Archivists,[3] and as far as internal records suggest, there were no events held in house at the AHC. It was evident that future involvement in any sort of Archives Month activities would require a minimal input of staff time to ensure that other AHC needs were not going unfulfilled.

The seed for what would become our 2012 Archives Month event was planted innocently enough in August 2011, when I attended a reception with faculty colleagues from other campus departments. As often happens whenever an archivist makes small talk with other academics, the conversation veered into "What exactly is it that you do?" territory. I have learned that it's just easier to talk about the collections that we make available to the public, and in this case, that turned out to be a happy accident. Upon learning that we have among our holdings the Forrest J. Ackerman papers, which contain a real, "live" tribble from the original *Star Trek* series episode "The Trouble with Tribbles,"[4] the faculty members were delighted. At the time two AHC staff members had curated an exhibit in the University of Wyoming Art Museum, "Terror in the Theater: Fifties Fears," and the tribble happened to be on display as a part of this exhibit. After inviting these faculty members to view the exhibit, they started an animated discussion about television shows from their childhoods. As the conversation progressed, one diminutive professor exclaimed, "What if you could win a date with the tribble?" The fervor with which professors were now describing their possible dinner outings with the tribble was infectious. I considered the idea in earnest, if only momentarily.

Now, while sending the tribble out on a date would have been quite an event indeed, it would have been rather awkward from a collection management perspective. Our materials don't circulate, like archives everywhere, and to allow an item to leave the building would require loan paperwork, insurance agreements, or perhaps even an AHC chaperone. Yes, talk about awkward! Also, tribbles are not known for their charming conversational abilities—even when animated, they only coo indiscriminately. The thought of a chaperoned dinner for the contest winner and his or her inanimate date, while hilarious, was impractical on multiple fronts. As a result, while I briefly considered the idea, it was quickly rejected and forgotten—until August 2012. With American Archives Month looming only two months away, the AHC was determined to participate in some fashion.

Ideas were solicited in departmental and advisory group meetings, and I introduced the possibility of doing something related to our fuzzy friend. It quickly became clear that nothing seemed to hold the cultural caché of the tribble. With the idea for "Win a Date with the Tribble" in the back of my mind, it became clear that if we were going to involve the tribble, we would have to do so in such a way as to limit any possible damage. Clearly, the artifact could not leave the building. How, then, could we entice people to take an interest in this item? There were so many tribbles in that *Star Trek* episode, and they were known by their collective name. What if we facilitated a contest so that our tribble could have a personal name? It seemed fairly straightforward at first. We would publicize the event through our blog and our Facebook and Twitter channels; judges would choose the winner and award a prize.

IMPLEMENTATION

The first difficulty that we encountered turned out to be the matter of what the prize might be. Initially, we thought that our entrants might all be local. A picture of the winner with the tribble seemed like an apt reward. However, in discussions with AHC administrators, it became clear that this option would not work. First, if winners were unable to come in person to be photographed, the "prize" would remain unawarded, which would negate any sense of success that our contest might generate—bad for morale and even worse PR. However, I was soon made aware of a more serious issue. As AHC director Mark Greene explained, "to post photos of the winner with the tribble on Facebook or YouTube . . . that kind of exploitation of the artifact would have increased our risk of run-in with the intellectual property holders. Whereas as long as we treated the tribble primarily as an artifact we happened to own, our risk was much less."[5] Then the concern was expressed that photographing the tribble at all might violate copyright restrictions because the rights to *Star Trek* are now held by CBS and Paramount Pictures. The option to send a photograph of the tribble for the winner to use as they might see fit could incur copyright violations, depending on how it was used.

Well, what to do? Mention copyright to most archivists, and as risk-averse individuals, we'll do anything in our power to avoid a lawsuit, especially with entities with much deeper financial reserves (such as Paramount). The contest almost completely ground to a halt at this point, which happened to be mid-September, just two weeks before the anticipated roll-out date of October 1. Instead, we decided to offer a more vague description of the prize to be awarded: "Winners receive a unique montage photograph of *Star Trek* memorabilia and full bragging rights!" This gave us some time to determine what would make a visually interesting reward for our participants. The montage photograph depicted several production stills and memorabilia from the original television show (archival items from the Forrest J. Ackerman collection) against a starry-night background.

An unanticipated challenge arose in assembling the panel of judges. A call for judges was issued to the Laramie Film Society, as well as to the local community through word of mouth, prior to the contest. However, while there was a lot of enthusiasm for the contest, it was a challenge to obtain firm commitments from individuals willing to serve as judges. The reasons for this remain unclear. Perhaps it was a busy time of the year, or maybe the idea of weighing in on such a cultural icon of science fiction was intimidating; regardless, we had thought that there would be no shortage of *Star Trek* aficionados who would be willing to evaluate the entries. Though this was not the case, the five judges were eventually secured. Three of the judges came from various departments at the AHC, one was a graduate student from the American Studies Department at the University of Wyoming, and one was an avid *Star Trek* fan and member of the Laramie community.

Having resolved the issues involved with awarding the prize but still frantically searching for judges, we set about with the launch of the contest. We announced it through our Facebook page on October 1, 2012, the first day of Archives Month. Originally, we had planned to use the AHC blog to publicize the contest as well, but within minutes of the Facebook post, we had our first entry, and others would follow in a flurry of *Star Trek* fervor, so we determined it was unnecessary to use our blog to publicize the contest. Our blog was supporting Archives Month in a different way, through the "Day in the Life" series (profiles of various archives staff members), and to be quite honest, we were already getting all the entries we could reasonably handle.

However, even though 795 people learned of the contest through our Facebook page, we have the Associated Press to thank for spreading the news of our contest nationally. The story was originally picked up through the AP's Cheyenne bureau. On October 3, I was contacted by an AP reporter to talk about the "Name the Tribble" contest, and we discussed the details and purpose behind it. On October 4, a University of Wyoming athletics event was taking place, and an AP reporter notified us that a photographer was already on his way to Laramie; he wanted to stop in at the AHC to get a photo of the tribble. The article[6] was already scheduled for release that day, and the photo would help in "giving this story wide play this morning."[7] Well, of course we said yes! Keith Reynolds, cocurator of the previous year's exhibit "Terror in the Theater: Fifties Fears," has the most knowledge of the tribble, as he processed the Forrest J. Ackerman papers, the collection in which the tribble resides. Luckily, he was available to pose with the tribble for a photo opportunity and could share his experience of encountering the tribble in the collection for the first time (see figure 9.1). After the AP story broke, other news organizations republished it, allowing us to reach a wider audience than we had thought possible. *The Huffington Post,*[8] *Salon,*[9] and *Yahoo! News*[10] are just several of the outlets that publicized our contest.

This unanticipated attention multiplied the number of responses we received—which was fantastic! However, it meant that we shied away from further advertising using our normal channels; it was a challenge to stay on top of the entries that we were already receiving. Initially, we tried to send a confirmation message to each and every entrant, either via

Figure 9.1.   Keith Reynolds with the tribble and the Forrest J. Ackerman papers in the American Heritage Center's reading room. Photo by Rick Walters.

e-mail or as a Facebook comment on their submission. It soon became impossible to respond individually, which is one of the unintended consequences that we discovered. This courtesy was regrettably abandoned, but as the sole facilitator of the contest, I was overwhelmed with keeping the entries and their authors in order, let alone acknowledging the receipt of entries.

We received a total of 454 entries from all over the United States and internationally. Entrants were invited to submit a tribble name via e-mail or by posting to our Facebook page. For e-mail entries we requested that entrants include their own names and their suggested tribble names in the subject line. When each entry was received, it was logged in an Excel spreadsheet. In addition to the name suggested, the method through which it was received, the name of the individual, and contact information for the contestant was recorded; it was also noted if there was accompanying documentation—book chapters, articles, or extensive reasoning behind the name entered.[11] We received entries through Facebook, e-mail, postal mail, and in person. In several cases individuals submitted more than one entry. The deadline of October 22 was enforced; no entries were considered if they were received after 11:59 p.m. on that date. The final and entire list of entries was then sent to the panel of five judges.

The judges were asked to review all entries prior to meeting on October 24, when they would choose five finalists. The winners were selected from a pool of 25 finalists out of the total of 454. The judges made arguments for their favorite entries, and a very civilized, collegial discussion ensued. Ultimately, five finalists were selected from the pool of twenty-five. The entries in this group of finalists demonstrate the creativity of our contestants, and the judges presented compelling cases for their favorites: "Serena" and "Alotta" embodied the most tribble-esque qualities (the tribbles' soothing effect on humans, as well as their rapid ability to reproduce); "Roddenhairy" cleverly punned on Gene Roddenberry's name— as the creator of the early *Star Trek* franchise, this seemed appropriate. "Wyomble" was another top contender, as this particular tribble now resides within the state of Wyoming. However, eventually the judges unanimously agreed that "Furry Ackerman" was the winner due to the clever connection with the archival collection in which the artifact is located. This name reflected the most visible physical attribute of the tribble, as well as paid homage to Forrest J. Ackerman. Because the intent of the contest was to provide a unique outreach avenue to increase awareness of archives and the work they do, as well as to promote the AHC's collections and services, this entry seemed to do the most toward achieving these goals.

Interestingly, two people had submitted the winning name, and we had no difficulty awarding credit to both. The winning entry was announced through the AHC blog later that day and reposted on Facebook and Twitter. The University of Wyoming's communications office announced the outcome of the contest through an online press release November 1, 2012. The *Billings Gazette*, the *Casper Star-Tribune*, and the *Gillette News Record* were among the newspapers that reported the results of the contest; several online news outlets reported the outcome as well, but ultimately media coverage about the results didn't match the buzz with which the launch of the contest had met.

Even though we attempted to spread the news of the contest results, our coverage area was much smaller than the national media outlets that had originally picked up the story. And, of course, it's easy to miss a small, one-off story in a newspaper or website, and there are no clues in subsequent days that would lead someone to follow up on the story. The wide media coverage was a blessing—it publicized the contest to more people than we could have if left to our usual devices. However, the coverage was a bit lopsided, tipping toward the start of the contest rather than its results.

The temporal characteristics of social media also contributed to many people missing the announcement of the results. Because posts are so fleeting—avoiding social media accounts for several days often means that one completely misses news items—infrequent or irregular use meant the results could simply be missed. Then, because of the constant need to update and refresh our social media presence, the AHC continued to post news items, so the announcement of the winning tribble name became buried under new content. The outcome of the contest also wasn't a news item that lent itself to frequent reposts, as event announcements and reminders do. One consequence of fewer reports on the outcome of the contest was that people still contact us (even at the end of March 2013) to ask if a name was ever chosen for the tribble—which also testifies to the appeal of the contest. These periodic inquiries regarding the contest results require only a minor investment of AHC resources and are a small price to pay for the free publicity that the contest generated for the institution.

RESULTS

The most visible, quantitative outcome measure for the "Name the Tribble" contest is the increased number of Facebook "likes" during and continuing even after the contest and the increased engagement and participation from this online audience. During the height of the contest, we had 423 people actively engaged with the contest—commenting on, sharing, and "liking" our posts or comments; we also managed to reach 7,537 people in total through Facebook alone—these were unique users who viewed our Facebook page. We received 174 entries via Facebook, compared with the 274 entries that were sent through e-mail. This indicates that traditional print media was extremely effective at communicating with our potential audience, though our internal efforts to publicize the contest on Facebook also reached a surprising number of online users.

The day prior to the launch of the contest, September 30, we had 175 Facebook "likes"; at the time of writing, we have 311. During the contest, we had 230 more, and we lost only two "likes" after the contest ended. Still, with our consistent efforts to post visually interesting news items, we have been able to build this number back up on the strength of our own merits rather than the popularity of the tribble itself. Since November 6, 2012, we have been steadily increasing our number of online followers at an average rate of one new "like" per week. The fact that we were able to retain the bulk of these new followers even after the tribble contest ended indicates that our day-to-day social media strategy is effective; our online audience continues to be receptive to the more ordinary news items that we post. In addition, certainly the volume of media coverage that we received bolstered the contest and raised the profile of the AHC both locally and nationally.

Although we have no baseline to compare it to, we feel that the sheer number of responses to our call for tribble name suggestions indicates that this particular online outreach effort was successful. However, we also know that much of this success was not due to our own efforts to advertise and publicize the event; we cannot take credit for the national media attention that the "Name the Tribble" contest received. We thought the tribble contest had the potential to stir up interest in the wider "Trekkie" community beyond our usual Wyoming history fans, and we were right! Still, the happy accident of the Associated Press learning of our Archives Month activity and publishing a story about it just days after the launch allowed us to reach a more diverse range of users.

Another measure of success of our increased online presence is that reference questions have begun to be submitted through our blog and Facebook pages. While we cannot trace this change in our user interactions directly to the tribble contest, there does seem to be a clear link: Prior to the "Name the Tribble Contest," we received a total of one question regarding the AHC's collections, and after the contest, we've received periodic reference questions submitted as direct messages or comments on our posts. I believe that our tribble contest presented a more accessible, approachable repository to the public; we also frequently respond to comments on our Facebook and blog pages, and I think this increased participation and activity on our part demonstrates how willing we are to engage with researchers of all levels.

Our success with this aspect of our overall online strategy—to engage more meaningfully with our users—is demonstrated by the questions we receive from our Facebook and blog pages. While nowhere near as frequent as the daily influx of reference questions to our reference department's e-mail address, we now receive inquiries at the rate of approximately one per month or every other month on our blog. What makes

this particularly interesting is that these questions come to us not immediately after the story is posted to our blog but weeks, months, or even a
year after the post is published. This asynchronous communication demonstrates that we are able to connect to our users where they are—when
they are searching for information on a particular topic, our resources are
there to support their research. Questions that we have received via our
Facebook page have varied from specific informational requests—for a
photograph, for instance—to more in-depth inquiries, such as whether a
certain collection contains a manual for a sewing machine model, or requests for family history information. These questions do appear to be
coming from new audience members; either before or after a question is
submitted through Facebook, the individual typically "likes" our page.
However, with the AHC's blog, it is less clear whether our readers have
been quietly reading for months or years or have just discovered us. Still,
our "regular customers" typically tend to call or e-mail reference staff
directly rather than asking questions through social media.

One concern at the outset of the contest was that the tribble would be
handled unnecessarily and would experience a more rapid degradation
in condition. However, as AHC collections manager William Hopkins
expressed it,

> For myself, I don't recall any real problems from a collection manage-
> ment standpoint. I never felt that the tribble was put at any particular
> risk during this process (it's not like we were letting people "walk" the
> tribble on a wire leash or something like that). . . . And the tribble was
> always used under controlled conditions so at no time was I particular-
> ly worried about damage to the artifact. Also, as artifacts go, this one is
> pretty robust and not prone to damage.[12]

Indeed, because so many of the participants in the contest were not in the
local area, we had only a few additional requests to view the tribble. In
2011, after the collection was processed and an online inventory made
available, there was only one request to view and handle the tribble; in
the months of 2012 that followed the contest, there were just three requests. Two of these requests were for publicity photographs for the
"Name the Tribble" contest, taken by the AHC's senior photographic
technician who is accustomed to working with fragile archival materials.

The tribble contest also raised other issues of collection security with
regard to this particular artifact. Hopkins indicated that the

> only new concern I was presented with was as a direct result of the
> unquestionable success of the contest. . . . [It] was due to the fact that 1)
> many more people now know we have a tribble in captivity, and 2) not
> long ago I read on a fan website that an original tribble like ours sold at
> auction for $4200. This put the tribble at a greater risk of theft, and so as
> a precaution I moved it into Restricted Access. That's really the only

additional precautions we've taken and it's probably something we should have done a long time ago. [13]

In this sense the tribble contest raised internal awareness of existing collections security issues and provided the AHC with an opportunity to address such issues.

LESSONS LEARNED

The AHC's experience with the "Name the Tribble" contest has produced a greater body of experience for everyone involved with the effort, from the AHC's administration to the collection management and reference departments. For archivists and managers contemplating various online outreach strategies, Mark Greene offers this advice: "Be willing to consider some risk in return for good publicity, good will, and improved image, but don't give up your responsibility of due diligence." [14] For those involved with the details of running a social media campaign, the issues of institutional reputation and responsibility can be easily overlooked because the logistics are the immediate focus. A review of the proposed activity by those in charge of managing an institution's reputation and mitigating any legal risks ensures a smoother process.

For any future contests, specifying one entry per person might help to reduce the amount of record keeping required—though it might result in more work for staff in that individuals' names would need to be checked against entries already received and might dampen some entrants' enthusiasm. Perhaps there is no elegant way to administer a contest with such wide publicity. Another key component we discovered is the need to ensure that the activity can easily increase in scale. While we managed to keep up with an overwhelming flow of contest entries, ensuring that we've implemented safeguards to avoid any sense of unpreparedness would most definitely keep the contest, as well as other core duties, running smoothly. In retrospect it might have been helpful to have another staff member or a volunteer help me with tracking and responding to the entries after the entries rapidly flooded the AHC's Facebook page and e-mail inbox rather than handling it all myself. Furthermore, automating the process of logging entries and sending receipt confirmation could be addressed by funneling all submissions through an online form that would automatically populate a spreadsheet and send a reply. Although, requiring people to submit entries through a form rather than by using more immediate channels like our Facebook page would take some of the spontaneity and interactivity out of the contest. Again, although the "more the merrier" approach encourages more interaction and participation, it does require more effort on the part of those supporting the contest. If outreach is the ultimate goal, it seems worth investing the resources if an event proves to be a hit.

We got lucky, too, in that our collection includes this cultural icon and in that the collection had been processed and I was aware of its existence—and ready to bring it up at a cocktail party and let the conversation inspire new ideas. A quick assessment of any archives' collections would provide a snapshot of what materials or artifacts might lend themselves to an online outreach strategy, too. Does the institution have among its holdings anything that might particularly capture the public's interest? Consult with fellow archivists; if someone on staff finds something especially interesting, chances are that others outside the profession will, too. In the case of the AHC, we were extremely fortunate to have a tribble among out holdings; however, there are less well-known items that could garner significant attention from a potential audience. Success can also depend on how your venture is designed to include the public; if our promotion of the tribble had been less interactive, I don't think we would have been able to capture the public's interest.

What is the best way to involve the archival material in a social media outreach effort? What are the goals of the outreach? All these are questions that will shape the direction the online outreach takes. In retrospect we at the AHC should have been more rigorous with our goals for our outreach effort; aside from attempting to demystify the archives and demonstrate the accessibility of our holdings, we didn't establish concrete objectives for the archives side of the archival awareness campaign. In the minds of those who participated, I'm sure that the fact that the tribble was part of the Forrest J. Ackerman papers was frequently overlooked and lost in the hubbub of fandom that surrounded the contest. While we attempted to emphasize the artifact's connection to the Ackerman collection at every possible juncture, that component of our message does not appear to have stuck.

While the finalists of the contest were pleased to receive their photo montage of *Star Trek* memorabilia, we didn't receive any feedback regarding the prize, its format, or its content. For all of the anxiety that it caused, the matter of the prize seemed to be a nonissue in the end. We had been concerned about providing adequate incentives to increase participation, however incentivizing our social media outreach strategies seems not to have had a significant impact. Our earlier efforts fell flat, not because of a lack of incentive, it was now clear, but because they were poorly conceived. For example, "Trivia Tuesdays" didn't allow for multiple responses and as a result were not inclusive. On the other hand, the tribble contest did not naturally impose constraints and was more inclusive, and it struck a nerve with the media and public. These are factors that the AHC will take into account when planning for our next large-scale online outreach activity.

Our experience with the media—good and bad—during the "Name the Tribble" contest taught us that we could have been more proactive about our approach. Based on this I recommend that, once the outreach strategy comes together, you should make sure that local media outlets know about the effort. Also, before the strategy is finalized, meet with your media contacts; they may have ideas to help improve your plan or further develop your publicity efforts. In addition, you can communicate what your institution *needs* from the news agency or media group. If the AHC had been able to maintain continuous contact with the various news outlets that published the announcement of the contest, for example, we would have been able to more widely publicize the results of the contest. In our case, the story about the launch of the contest was disseminated so widely that we couldn't keep track of all of the newspapers and online news websites in which it appeared. Approaching specific individuals at media outlets ensures that your institution can, in some part, control the message.

CONCLUSION

The AHC's experimentation with the "Name the Tribble" contest emerged out of our ongoing efforts to engage with existing users and to attract new audiences to our collections and services. Our experience with the contest demonstrated the benefits of taking reasonable risks with our outreach efforts. By taking a new approach and incorporating a high-interest artifact into our outreach effort, we were able to reach those who were unfamiliar with the AHC's collections and services. Indeed, through our social media strategies, we've been able to retain most of this audience that discovered us on these social media channels during the contest. As a result we have consciously created a specific online personality, developed in part through our experience with the tribble contest. Our online persona is quirky, upbeat, and attuned to current events happening nationally as well as regionally and replies to all those who comment on our posts. I believe that this last component is crucial—it demonstrates that we're paying attention and confirms that there is a real person on the other end of the screen. In order to take this further, we may wish to sign each post with the name of the AHC contributor, however at the moment this has not become an issue, as I am the sole manager of the AHC's social media streams.

The "Name the Tribble" contest also underscored the importance of interdepartmental communication to express concerns and adequate time to assess potential risks. Many of the issues that nearly derailed the contest prior to its public launch could have been avoided had we allowed more time to work through them and run the concept of the "Name the Tribble" contest through a structured vetting process. Still, our success with this effort has demonstrated to internal stakeholders the importance of participating in similar online outreach campaigns in the future. There are other unique items that lurk in our collections that we hope to use in future online outreach efforts, and we'll be able to incorporate the crucial takeaways from the "Name the Tribble" contest into these future efforts. Social media tools continue to evolve, and so will the AHC's social media persona—we have learned that this evolution is an adventure to be embraced, much like those intrepid crew members of the starship *Enterprise* who embarked on their otherworldly explorations with anticipation and optimism.

Rachel Dreyer *is assistant reference archivist at the American Heritage Center, University of Wyoming.*

NOTES

1. American Heritage Center, *Web 2.0 Task Force Report*, June 2010.
2. This was prior to 2006, when the Society of American Archivists began supporting a national publicity campaign for Archives Month in 2006.
3. "American Heritage Center 2009–2010 Annual Report," *American Heritage Center*, accessed June 14, 2013, http://www.uwyo.edu/ahc/_files/annual-reports/ahc-annual-report-2009-10.pdf.
4. For those readers who may not be familiar with tribbles, they are living, cooing, purring balls of fur. They are hermaphroditic and can reproduce extremely rapidly. They have a special penchant for the quadrotritricale, a type of grain. In addition, they possess other unique characteristics—for example, tribbles have a soothing effect on humans but are the mortal enemies of Klingons everywhere. In the "Trouble with Tribbles" episode, Lieutenant Uhura receives a tribble as a gift from space trader Cyrano Jones. It multiplies rapidly, soon taking over every available space on the ship. They find their way into a cargo hold containing the quadrotritricale grain bound for a distant planet. The tribbles soon devour all the grain, but many soon begin to die off, which exposes a Klingon plot to poison the grain. Surviving tribbles also help identify the Klingon saboteur on board the ship. See http://www.imdb.com/title/tt0708480 for more information about the episode.
5. Mark Greene, e-mail message to author, April 10, 2013.
6. Mead Gruver, "Wyoming Tribble-Naming Contest Marks Archives Month," *Casper Star Tribune*, October 4, 2012, http://trib.com/news/state-and-regional/wyoming-tribble-naming-contest-marks-archives-month/article_3e59995b-26a5-50be-a375-ab7cd0159f9f.html.
7. Mead Gruver, e-mail message to author, October 4, 2012.
8. Mead Gruver, "Name the Tribble Contest: 'Star Trek' Creature Featured in American Archives Month Promotion," *Huffington Post* [New York], October 4, 2012, http://www.huffingtonpost.com/2012/10/05/name-tribble-contest-star-trek-american-archives-month_n_1942099.html.
9. Mead Gruver, "Wyo. Tribble-Naming Contest Marks Archives Month," *Salon* [San Francisco], October 4, 2012, http://www.salon.com/2012/10/04/wyo_tribble_naming_contest_marks_archives_month.
10. Mead Gruver, "Univ. of Wyo.'s American Heritage Center Holds Contest to Name Tribble from Star Trek Set," *Yahoo! TV* [Sunnyvale, CA], October 4, 2012, http://tv.yahoo.com/news/wyo-tribble-naming-contest-marks-archives-month-203347481.html.
11. For example, we received extensive explanations of Klingon vocabulary and translations, as well as many entries that based their reasoning upon "facts" from the *Star Trek* series, the specific episode in which the tribbles appeared, and trivia from the late 1960s sci-fi culture from which *Star Trek* emerged.

12. William Hopkins, e-mail message to author, April 12, 2013.
13. Ibid.
14. Greene.

TEN

Navigating Nightingale

Creating an App Out of Archives

Geoff Browell, King's College London

In September 2010, King's College London launched Navigating Nightingale, an iPhone walking tour app of central London following the course of the River Thames and retracing the life of the pioneering nurse and public health reformer Florence Nightingale. The release of the app coincided with the centenary of Nightingale's death and the 150th anniversary of the opening of the Florence Nightingale School of Nursing at King's, the world's first nurse-training academy. The app was developed collaboratively by King's College London Archives, King's School of Nursing, the AIM25 partnership, and Centre Screen, a multimedia production company that focuses on the museum and heritage sectors.[1]

This was my first experience of developing an app. Since then apps have grown to become an integral part of the cultural landscape. Popular apps have been developed by large public museums and visitor attractions to improve access to art exhibitions or showcase new collections, growing out of existing expertise in audio or self-guided technology.[2] These organizations have the advantage of rich content, a captive market, and experience of developing games and interactive visitor displays that can be easily translated into apps. Archive apps, however, are a more challenging proposition, not least because of the potential difficulty of representing archival documents on small screens. This chapter covers the main aspects of the development of just such an archive app, including the rationale, picture research, technical features, and lessons learned.

PLANNING

King's College London was founded in 1829 and is a leading research and teaching university. Its archives[3] contain a wealth of material on the arts, humanities, sciences, and medicine, including major inventions and discoveries, such as the development of the first electric telegraph and experiments to decipher the DNA double helix during the 1950s. While primarily a research archive, it attracts visits and inquiries from all over the world, including from college alumni, high school students, filmmakers, and journalists.

The archives have long been committed to improving public access via catalogs, online exhibitions, and digitization. It was among the first, in 1996, to publish detailed catalogs online. These have recently been relaunched using ARCHIOS software, which facilitates the enhancement of catalogs with images, timelines, and linked open data.[4] Our drive to encourage new audiences to engage with archival sources similarly provided the inspiration for a project using theatrical reinterpretation of archives relating to the history of British military involvement in Afghanistan in the late nineteenth century to support the training of soldiers being deployed there in the present day.[5]

King's College Archives set up AIM25 in 2000 and still manages the service. AIM25 is an archival description aggregator for more than 140 London-based archives that allows users to cross-search some 17,000 descriptions spanning more than 500 years of history covering themes as diverse as politics, war, geography, literature, science, medicine, and technology. New content and partners are added regularly, and the site attracts more than 1 million hits per month from researchers across the globe, including scholars, students, family historians, and the media.[6]

Since its inception AIM25 has sought to utilize new technology to make archives more accessible. Recently, this commitment culminated in a series of projects to develop linked open data editing tools to support the aggregation of archive, library, museum, and heritage content in association with the international catalog software vendor Axiell and the historical mapping specialist Historypin. The objective has been to connect relevant content and enhance otherwise flat and uninspiring catalog descriptions, for example, through their display on map interfaces.[7]

AIM25 is also always looking to build new audiences for archival material, and this inspired the walking tour concept, conceived as a new and exciting way of attracting younger and more curious visitors to archives and moving beyond the traditional constituencies of academics, professional researchers, and genealogists. The aim was to break down the barriers by taking archives beyond the search room to busy people on the move. However, while tourists and casual visitors understandably flock to London's museums and art galleries, they are less familiar with the presence of world-leading archives and still less able to appreciate the potential of their photographs and other holdings to inspire, educate, and entertain.

The archives recognized the potential of apps as a fruitful medium of public engagement soon after they began to enter the public consciousness with the opening of Apple's app store in 2008. As we saw it, the app could provide a mobile shop window in which geographically linked surrogates of archival materials can be shared both with visitors to a city or region equipped with a smartphone or tablet or by people from the comfort of their own homes. The broader potential of cultural apps was that, when combined with digitized content and crowdsourced knowledge about places and events, apps could enhance catalogs and connect stories about the human and natural environments in new ways. Rich visualizations and gamification of archive sources would also become possible, again building whole new audiences for historical material.

In due course we have seen that apps can also support institutions' teaching programs, for example, through the release of copies of popular but inaccessible documents by the U.S. National Archives as "Today's Document."[8] The remorseless rise of the smartphone to market dominance and the emergence of the iPad and other tablet devices have fueled growing public demand for apps: 50 billion apps had been downloaded from the Apple app store alone by May 2013. At the same time, the availability of content management system (CMS)–style app-creation platforms and the introduction of hybrid HTML5 solutions have further brought app publication within the range of cultural organizations with comparatively small budgets.[9]

In 2010, however, there were few precedents for the creation of a walking tour app with a library, archive, museum, or cultural focus. The Museum of London had successfully launched its popular Street Museum during the development of Navigating Nightingale.[10] This augmented reality app uses Google Maps to overlay modern and historical images of places in London. Historypin launched its beta version at the same time.[11] Both apps used the augmented approach to history that Navigating Nightingale sought to exploit for its potential to inspire engagement with popular history. It was hoped that the shock of seeing the new overlaying the old would provide a vivid new way of recreating a lost London and allow users to connect emotionally with their neighborhood and its stories.

The theme of the Navigating Nightingale app was inspired just as much by convenient timing as anything else; we were searching for an appropriate theme for our first app just as the Nightingale anniversary was approaching. The project thus arose less from the overriding desire to celebrate the life of Nightingale and more from a tradition of innovation and experimentation in outreach at King's College Archives: blending a focus on the user with a serendipitous exploitation of networks of expertise and emerging technological opportunities.

IMPLEMENTATION

AIM25 is primarily a partnership of research institutions, and it was understood that the proposed app would be underpinned by rigorous academic input. The archives had a mature working relationship with the School of Nursing and Midwifery at King's, where student nurses have the opportunity to take a module exploring how the profession has evolved historically. Students draw on rich archival holdings to support their study, including late nineteenth-century syllabuses and examination questions; the diaries of student nurses; recipe and drug books; records of wards detailing patient care in London hospitals; newspaper cuttings; wartime photograph albums; and surviving artifacts, like uniforms and equipment for dispensing medicine.

Serendipitously, partnership between the archives and the School of Nursing supplied the theme for the app: the 150th anniversary of the School of Nursing and centenary of the death Florence Nightingale.[12] A historical conference and exhibition on the theme of Nightingale in autumn 2010 provided a convenient launch deadline. The school's project partner and historical advisor, Dr. Rosemary Wall, a specialist in public health and the history of nursing, took charge of assembling a broad range of archival content from a number of AIM25 partner institutions that was anticipated would include letters, photographs, illustrations, diaries, printed publications, sound recordings, maps, and moving pictures. One of the aspirations of the project team was to experiment with the technology necessary to display a variety of document types, and this informed our initial selections.

Research took longer than expected. A basic search on AIM25 yields a summary of partner archives that hold material on Nightingale and the history of nursing, but we knew the app would address other themes, including the histories of war, public health, and the city of London. In order to provide a rounded account of Nightingale's life, other historical content from archives that are not part of the AIM25 network had to be accessed. We used our existing contacts within the nursing-history, archival, and history-of-London communities, and, where necessary, picture libraries. Selection was based on historical relevance and on locating striking signature images that tell a story at a glance.

A key question quickly arose from preliminary research: Should the app be driven by the historical narrative or by the archival content, or should the story and content be selected to fit the technology? In practice, a mixed economy prevailed. The app graphic design team, its developers, and the historian and archivist quickly reached agreement on the main outlines of Nightingale's life, which provided the sections into which the app is subdivided. Deeper research yielded interesting but less well-known detail, not least about the buildings that lined the route of the app. AIM25 archivists volunteered unexpected items that required rethinking aspects of the design, such as a late-Victorian flip-book that gives the illusion of moving traffic in Trafalgar Square in the 1890s. The developers and designers for their part made design suggestions, such as a cartoon showing street characters that they were keen to show "coming to life" with voice and song, and this required the historian and archivist to try to locate a good example. The depiction of archive documents on a small screen poses singular difficulties, and on the whole Navigating Nightingale sought to avoid using digital copies, preferring transcription and narration, though the example of the John Murray Archive app from the National Library of Scotland shows how this can be achieved successfully.[13]

The selection of the developers and designers proved to be easier than expected. As the manager of AIM25, I made contact with Centre Screen at a London trade show. Centre Screen is a company that develops educational exhibitions for visitor and museum attractions. Its focus on high production values, scriptwriting, and research of target audiences aligned with the preoccupation at King's with the storytelling approach to archives and stress on the user experience. Centre Screen was keen to augment its offer to existing customers with apps containing exciting and original content, and to do this they generously donated their time. Centre Screen focused on storyboarding the app, designing its feature set, developing graphic design, editing and recording its sound effects and accompanying commentary, and overseeing its technical development. Centre Screen's developers would ensure technical compliance with Apple and register the completed app with the Apple app store. [14]

The project team made an early commitment to focus development using the iOS operating system for the iPhone. The open-source Android operating system was in its infancy, and Centre Screen only had the resources to focus on one native development. Another important decision was to protect users from costly roaming charges by ensuring that the app could be downloaded complete and did not require streaming or syncing of video or other content. This decision placed a maximum realistic size on the app and its constituent content and features.

A strategic decision was also reached to adopt the so-called freemium model and publish the app for free in its first version, with expected upgrades and additional features available for a modest charge. This arose from careful analysis of competitor apps and the desire to encourage immediate use of the app to kick-start the development of a series of companion apps that would be competitively priced.

The use of QR codes to allow curious passersby to download the app was rejected on the grounds that they were little used at the time and that obtaining permission for their attachment to such street furniture as bus stops would potentially prove too time consuming and costly to negotiate with the owners. Lastly, it was agreed that the app should be the first in a series on the theme of medicine and health dubbed "Medical

Milestones." A strong brand identity was sought with the creation of a blue-and-white "road sign" logo. With hindsight, this proved confusing to potential customers and was soon superseded by the home screen of the app with its colorful navigation wheel (see figure 10.1).

Navigating Nightingale was only made possible because most work was carried out for free, except for some necessary image reproduction and rights fees. Generally, however, archives were happy to supply copies of images in return for publicity and association with an innovative project. While many archives have a scale of charges for traditional book, journal, broadcast, or online publication, this was not true of publication via an app, and the project encountered delays while appropriate fees structures were negotiated for the first time.

The selection of the route provided the first challenge for the development team. Nightingale's life and career can be traced from her birth in the Italian city that bears her name through education and service throughout the world, most famously during the Crimean War (1853–1856), when Nightingale earned her public reputation as the "lady with the lamp," administering to the needs of sick and injured soldiers at

Figure 10.1.   Screencaps showing the home screen of the app, with the navigation wheel, and the "Florence's Friends" feature.

the hospital at Scutari. While content displayed on any prospective route needed to make reference to her travels and the range of her experience, it necessarily was required to focus on her subsequent career in London, where she sought to exercise political influence to improve the provision of public health through changes to government policy and where a school of nursing was set up at St. Thomas' Hospital in London.

The team explored a number of possible routes before agreeing on a circular tour from King's College London along the banks of the Thames. Stopping points were located strategically along the way at intervals of several hundred yards. Each provided the user with a vantage point from which to view London with a fresh perspective and, in so doing, progressively learn more about Nightingale, her achievements, and her legacy. Each stopping point corresponded with a different aspect of Nightingale's life relevant to the buildings in the vicinity. Hence her work on innovative, more hygienic hospital design was brought to the fore during the St. Thomas' Hospital stop, while her career as a political lobbyist was highlighted in a stop outside the Houses of Parliament. Similarly, her role as a health care reformer in wartime was stressed during the stops outside the modern Ministry of Defence building in Whitehall.

The use of stopping points also provided the opportunity for users to join the route at any point and still complete the entire tour or only the parts that most interested them. New display features were introduced at each stop. These arose iteratively from the need to showcase specific examples of archive content appropriate to that location. One common feature across the whole route was the augmented reality that accompanied "then and now" views of buildings along the route, which we dubbed "historical X-ray."

Navigation can pose problems for apps, as rich historical and other content can take up too much space, making the app unfeasibly large to download and prone to bugs. The designers were therefore forced to think laterally to overcome these problems while retaining an immersive experience that was nevertheless stable, robust, and intuitive to use.

A one-minute introduction provides a snappy opening commentary on Nightingale's education, career, and achievements. This is accompanied by moving footage of London's Trafalgar Square in the late nineteenth century, with atmospheric sound effects of horses' hooves to draw the user into the imagined world of Nightingale at around the time of the birth of cinema. The footage derived from the chance discovery in the archives of the Institution of Engineering and Technology of a flip-book, a type of picture book whose pages can be agitated to give the illusion of movement, which was popular in the 1890s. The introduction leads onto the centerpiece of the app: the "coxcomb" wheel that provides the app's start screen and iconic reference to Nightingale's own work as a statistician. It was Nightingale herself who invented the coxcomb diagram as a lobbying tool to persuade Queen Victoria and the British government to improve sanitation in military hospitals. The original diagram, a mix of bar and pie charts, features sectors that project out from the center of the chart (mimicking the fleshy fanlike headpieces found on chickens and turkeys after which this type of diagram is named), which Nightingale used to illustrate the monthly death toll of soldiers owing to poor hygiene. The designers drew inspiration from the diagram to build an almost-circular wheel navigation resembling a pie chart divided into nine segments. Each provides fingertip access to a chapter of the story that corresponds in turn with a stopping point on the route. The coxcomb provided an elegant navigation tool, an enduring reference to this aspect of Nightingale's achievements, and an arresting signature image for use in subsequent publicity for the app.

Subsequent stops then showcase a range of design features and historical content. "Call to Crimea" invites the user to pause on the river terrace of Somerset House, the imposing complex of eighteenth-century public buildings adjacent to King's College that housed the Navy Office during the time of the Crimean War. A slide show and accompanying narration previews a series of contemporary paintings of the site. In common with the other segments, each illustration is accompanied by a short caption and picture credits, providing an additional layer of contextual information and replacing the commentary if noisy traffic makes it difficult to follow. The stop also introduces a lighthearted "Did you know?" diversion, which provides a number of usually humorous or fascinating historical facts designed to broaden the appeal of the app to those with a general interest in London.

The user is prompted to walk onto Waterloo Bridge. This provides the first use of the augmented reality slider bar, the "historical X-ray." The feature, which resembles a vertical timeline, was developed to allow users to adjust the opacity to transition between contemporary and historical photograph overlays. The intended effect is for the user to adopt the role of archival time-traveler. The user can swing through 360 degrees and use the slider to reveal otherwise-invisible features, which in this case include photographs of a brewery, dockyards, and a shot tower for making lead bullets. These examples of industrial architecture common on the south bank of the Thames in central London, which survived until the clearances after World War II, would no doubt have been familiar to Nightingale and would have been typical of the workplaces of many of her patients. The purpose here is to provide context to the story of health care in a London of poverty and manual employment.

The slider also reveals the now-demolished entrance to the Kingsway Tram Tunnel on the north side of the river. Tunnels are a common feature of the app: Exploration of underground London is consistent with the addition of quirky and eccentric features that mirror the variety and eclecticism of London's archive collections, a taster of the historical treasure hunt that would await a visitor who has been inspired by the app to pay a visit to real collections and delve into their secrets.

The next stop, themed around the problem of Victorian London's poverty and illness, explores the potential of map overlays for combining different types of historical data. Digital copies of poverty maps drawn up by the social reformer Charles Booth between 1886 and 1903 were obtained from the London School of Economics.[15] The maps describe, street by street, the extremes of wealth and poverty present in London at the turn of the century in vivid and shocking detail. The maps are then overlaid with extracts from the patient case notes of children suffering serious infectious diseases, drawn from data held by Great Ormond Street Children's Hospital. These had previously been prepared by a team of historians and volunteers at Kingston University as part of the Historic Hospital Admission Records Project, a study of records chronicling child health and childhood diseases. The resulting map highlights the link between deprivation and illness among the youth of Nightingale's London and a poignant reminder of the fragility of life in a nineteenth-century industrial metropolis.

The value of an illustration in telling a story is explored in the next stop, "Popular Reputation." Here, Centre Screen designers animated a colorful Victorian cartoon depicting an array of Dickensian street characters with accompanying music and poetry to reflect upon Nightingale's celebrity and her reception in popular culture. The School of Nursing's choir recorded accompanying songs in the style of late Victorian popular music. Once again, the purpose here is to surprise the user with an unusual or unexpected feature while communicating a serious historical message.

"Hospitals" moves the user to Westminster Bridge overlooking St. Thomas' Hospital and Parliament. The "historical X-ray" feature tells the story of Nightingale's influence on hospital design with the objective of a healthier and more hygienic environment for patients. The stop also tells the story of the Palace of Westminster and of the fire that destroyed its medieval predecessor in 1834. The importance of using bold and colorful images to capture the attention of the app user is brought home at this juncture, with the employment of dramatic contemporary oil paintings showing the course of the conflagration. Variety in the selection of archival content proved crucial to sustaining interest, along with the need to obtain large, high-resolution copies of archival documents to enable designers to amplify vivid or telling details.

The next two stops, "Legislation" and "Religion," both revert to using a conventional slide show of historical images describing the political and ethical legacy of Nightingale. The penultimate stop focuses on the Embankment constructed along the banks of the Thames to protect the city against flooding. Here, a remarkable recent discovery is incorporated: private photography of daily life captured by the playwright George

Bernard Shaw and available for the first time as a result of a major digitization project carried out by the London School of Economics Archives.[16] The final stage completes the tour with a wax cylinder recording of Nightingale's own voice, which is one of the oldest surviving examples of its kind.

In addition to the main tour, the app also provides access to a feature called "Nightingale's Friends," a Facebook-like portrait gallery of the famous and not-so-famous contemporaries of Nightingale (see figure 10.1) mentioned throughout the app to which users could refer by stepping out of the tour at any time. Along with the "Friends" feature, a Google Maps option is always present in the footer bar to facilitate orientation and identify each of the stopping points.

RESULTS

The app was launched in association with a public exhibition and a conference on Nightingale's life and career held at King's College and the Wellcome Library. The events also provided constructive interim feedback on the design of the app through the distribution of comments forms. The app was subsequently promoted via the archives, School of Nursing, Florence Nightingale Museum, AIM25, and Centre Screen's own website. A flyer was mailed out to interested parties, including Departments of the History of Science and Medicine, while articles written on the project include one in *History Today*, the leading U.K. popular history journal.[17] Since its launch I have given a number of promotional talks at public conferences on the broader potential of apps in the heritage sector. These focus on the practical hurdles and provide encouragement to other archivists looking to develop their own apps.

The response has been very positive from within the organization as a successful example of innovation and outreach. Interest from the public in the project led directly to further work to exploit King's rich holdings on the history of nursing, beginning with a volunteer project to create a database and website of the first 10,000 professional nurses active in the late nineteenth century. These nurses were members of the Royal British Nurses' Association, whose archive at King's contains a wealth of personal information about their education, training, family and social circumstances, and consequent careers.[18] Further medical and nursing apps are planned, with apps being one output in a broader strategy of community engagement that includes exhibitions, schools outreach, and public health awareness using historic archives.

Between launch in September 2010 and January 2014, the app was downloaded 763 times. On average 60 percent of users are from the United Kingdom and 20 percent from the United States. A variety of other countries make up the list, including China, Germany, Australia, and

Japan. The relatively low download statistics might at first appear disappointing in comparison with online search metrics but arguably not if an app of this kind is viewed in the same context as a book or other specialist publication.

Feedback is vital for this kind of project, and the first designs included features for capturing user opinion, but these were dropped before the final release due to lack of time. Ideally, similar projects should include a longer testing phase to iron out problems, not least through mystery shopper–style exercises and online surveys. There was no evidence from the project of an increase in user numbers to the archives concerned following the publication of the app, though it is possible that this may have happened. The capture of statistics on the motivation of users of archives provided by such surveys as the Public Services Quality Group or the U.K. Archives Discovery Network in the United Kingdom is insufficiently granular to tease out this kind of detail about the value of catalogs, engagement, or translational impact, a deficiency that might need to be addressed as dissemination technologies become more diverse.[19]

LESSONS LEARNED

While the app was actively promoted, a central lesson is that a project of this kind does not sell itself. In this respect it is like any other website, product, or service. Its purpose needs to be clearly defined and a general marketing and promotional plan developed, while retaining the space to exploit unexpected opportunities for dissemination when they arise. For us creating the app was in itself an experiment and served in some ways as its own reward, so in our case the relatively slow public uptake of the app was not a problem. In retrospect, we had developed very few measures to assess whether the app we had actually created was successful.

However, meaningful assessment ought to be central to any planning for such a project in order to help demonstrate value to stakeholders and provide a platform for successful fund raising to build new apps. Feedback can also be assembled to improve the performance of the app and schedule improvements into new releases. App store download statistics are a useful measure of success, but Navigating Nightingale shows that cultural apps can take time to build up recognition and visibility, and this rarely happens overnight. Relatively low download statistics like Navigating Nightingale's shouldn't deter potential developers of archive apps. While all but the most modest return on investment is unlikely except in the case of popular "breakout" apps that capture the public imagination, the app can instead serve as an extension to an existing outreach or marketing strategy and support other funded initiatives, such as digitization, building partnerships with researchers and attracting institutional encouragement that opens further avenues of investment and support.

Archivists should begin by asking a searching question. Do they need an app, or can the desired result be achieved more cost effectively by some other means? Similarly, simply reproducing a desktop experience on a small mobile screen probably isn't sensible. Apps work best for people on the move, with time to spare, or because they meet some perceived or practical need. The most successful recent apps in the cultural or heritage sector are ones that are both accessible and useful, which is why walking tours containing historical content or stories or the augmenting and enriching of museum or art or other exhibitions make for popular and successful products. Examples include the award-winning "Sound Uncovered" from the Exploratorium in San Francisco, which explores the history of sound, or the "Europeana" app, aggregating content from Europe's museums and archives.[20]

The choice of operating system and supported device is the most important technology decision to be taken prior to the commencement of a project. This influences the feature set, target audience, projected sales, and budget. When Navigating Nightingale was conceived, the Android market was in its infancy. This is no longer true, and it can be potentially costly to retrospectively convert content and features designed for different platforms that use very different programming languages. Cross-platform development ought to be considered at the earliest opportunity.

The recent adoption of HTML5, which provides for the delivery of the app experience in a web environment, is one option and, for a simple and uncomplicated app, might be sufficient. Responsive web design, which enables the optimal viewing of content on a variety of devices, including tablets and mobiles, can provide the appearance of a simple app at a fraction of the cost. A cheaper alternative still is to use the many subscription-based platforms that provide templates for publishing basic apps to accompany such events as exhibition launches. [21] However, it probably remains true that native coding in one or more of the main mobile operating systems is still required if the intention is to deliver a truly immersive experience that shows off archive content to best effect.

In terms of actual design and logistics, the most complex challenges reflected the use of images on the screen of a small mobile device, including finding room for necessary captioning and credit lines. The "historical X-ray" feature also proved difficult to implement, as it depended on the availability of a continuity of images across time to make possible the augmented reality effect with its characteristic ghosting of photographs. Unexpected technical challenges included the length of time taken for developer registration and app store approval. License registration also lapsed, resulting in the temporary removal of the app from the app store. An important lesson is that an app requires ongoing technical management and promotion to maintain its currency and viability, and the costs of ensuring such sustainability need to be factored into any medium or long-term financial calculations.

CONCLUSION

While the creation of the Navigating Nightingale app was initially sparked by our desire to explore new technology, based on my experience, I believe that a strong story and consistent narrative should arguably take precedence over the selection of technology. In our case we were to base our app on a famous lead character, public familiarity with Nightingale's achievements, and the setting of a historically diverse global city. As this chapter demonstrates, building a high-quality app requires careful preparation, high production values (particularly in graphic design and the recording of accompanying music or narration), and proper storyboarding and caption writing. The most persuasive reason for beginning an app project is because there is an important story that needs telling for which a mobile app is the most appropriate vehicle. Otherwise a desktop exhibition, resource pack, conference, or blended-learning approach might be a more suitable form of dissemination. The Nightingale story worked well as an app because of the variety of content we were able to assemble and our choice to center it around a walking tour, thus allowing us to take advantage of a sequence of physical features—in our case buildings—that are enjoyed to best effect on a mobile device by visitors to London. Not all places or archives collections will be as rich in potential, but a well-thought-through app can overcome these deficiencies and highlight previously unknown tales, people, and places. In either event care ought to be taken to avoid gimmickry that might distract the user or dilute the core historical message. While we explored using a variety of techniques to tell our story, we feel that all of them contributed effectively to bringing the story to life.

The growing importance of the app and ubiquity of the smartphone and tablet are difficult for cultural institutions to ignore. However, the potential cost and a propensity to play safe can diminish the impact of the cultural or archival app, hence recent criticisms of what have been described as "boring" museum apps.[22] The future of the technology arguably lies in blending the app with other types of learning, for example, to develop games that use collections in innovative ways, collect new information from users that can facilitate cocuration of collections, or provide an interface between the virtual and physical environments of the search room or museum gallery. Augmentation with content provides a new avenue for the appreciation of archival documents: One possible use would be in Google Glass or other personalized device applications to embed or overlay photographs, commentary, or other content from archives into a streetscape or in controlled environments, including museums, historic buildings, or such outdoor spaces as historic battlefields. More practical apps to help the archivist and researcher might include transcription, translation, and handwriting recognition of documents. Ultimately, apps, like other methods of outreach, provide an opportunity for the custodians of collections to create, innovate, inspire, and engage in order to build new audiences for the future.

Geoff Browell *is the senior archives services manager, King's College London.*

NOTES

1. Centre Screen Productions Ltd., "Navigating Nightingale," *iTunes Preview*, accessed June 26, 2013, https://itunes.apple.com/us/app/navigating-nightingale/id420890908?mt=8.

2. Examples of archival apps include New York Public Library apps, accessed July 14, 2013, http://www.nypl.org/mobile-help; "Europeana Open Culture," accessed July 15, 2013, https://itunes.apple.com/us/app/europeana-open-culture/id646414251?mt=8.

3. "Archives and Special Collections," *King's College London*, accessed January 28, 2014, http://www.kcl.ac.uk/library/collections/archivespec/index.aspx.

4. "Archios," *Imagiz*, accessed June 26, 2013, http://www.imagiz.com/archios.

5. "Fighting Your Corner," *King's College London*, accessed June 26, 2013, http://www.kingscollections.org/servingsoldier/collection/fighting-your-corner.

6. *AIM25*, accessed June 30, 2013, http://www.aim25.ac.uk.

7. *AIM25 Step Change and Open Metadata Pathway*, accessed June 30, 2013, http://openmetadatapathway.blogspot.co.uk.

8. "Today's Document App," *National Archives and Records Administration*, accessed October 30, 2013, http://www.archives.gov/social-media/todays-doc-app.html.

9. Roberto Baldwin, "Apple Hits 50 Billion Apps Served," *Wired*, May 15, 2013, http://www.wired.com/gadgetlab/2013/05/apple-hits-50-billion-served. App CMS platforms include the App Builder (http://www.theappbuilder.com). Examples of richer, gamelike experiences include "Phone Booth" from the London School of Economics (http://phone.booth.lse.ac.uk).

10. "Streetmuseum," *Museum of London*, accessed June 30, 2013, http://www.museumoflondon.org.uk/Resources/app/you-are-here-app/home.html.

11. *Historypin*, accessed June 30, 2013, http://www.historypin.com. Other examples include "Powerhouse Museum Walking Tours," *iTunes Preview*, accessed June 30, 2013, https://itunes.apple.com/au/app/powerhouse-museum-walking/id442064581?mt=8; and "Circa," accessed June 30, 2013, http://circaapp.com.

12. "Florence Nightingale School of Nursing: About the School: History," *King's College London*, accessed June 30, 2013, http://www.kcl.ac.uk/nursing/about/history.aspx.

13. "John Murray Archive App," *National Library of Scotland*, accessed July 20, 2013, http://www.nls.uk/murray-app.

14. *Centre Screen Productions*, accessed June 27, 2013, http://www.centrescreen.co.uk.

15. "Charles Booth Online Archive," *London School of Economics and Political Science*, accessed July 20, 2013, http://booth.lse.ac.uk; "Welcome to HHARP, the Home of 19th Century Children's Hospital Records," *Historic Hospital Admission Records Project*, accessed July 20, 2013, http://www.hharp.org.

16. "Shaw Photographs" *London School of Economics*, accessed February 17, 2014, , http://archives.lse.ac.uk/Record.aspx?src=CalmView.Catalog&id=SHAW+PHOTOGRAPHS.

17. Nicola Phillips, "Family History: Calling Up Your Ancestors," *History Today* 62, no. 6 (2012), http://www.historytoday.com/nicola-phillips/family-history-calling-your-ancestors.

18. "Pioneering Nurses," *King's College London*, accessed July 20, 2013, http://www.kingscollections.org/nurses/home.

19. "Public Services Quality Group (PSQG)," *Archives and Records Association: UK and Ireland*, accessed July 20, 2013, http://www.archives.org.uk/si-psqg/public-services-quality-group-psqg.html; "Resources," *UKAD*, accessed July 20, 2013, http://www.ukad.org/resources/index.html.

20. Exploratorium, "Sound Uncovered," *iTunes Preview*, accessed October 15, 2013, https://itunes.apple.com/us/app/sound-uncovered/id598835017?mt=8; Glimworm IT BV, "Europeana Open Culture," *iTunes Preview*, accessed October 15, 2013, https://itunes.apple.com/us/app/europeana-open-culture/id646414251?mt=8.

21. Examples include "Buzztouch," accessed July 20, 2013, http://www.buzztouch.com; and "Appsbar," accessed July 20, 2013, http://www.appsbar.com.

22. Mairin Kerr, "Are Museum Apps Boring?" *edgital*, August 8, 2013, http://www.edgital.org/2013/08/08/are-museum-apps-boring.

ELEVEN

DIY History

Redesigning a Platform for a Transcription Crowdsourcing Initiative

Jen Wolfe and Nicole Saylor, University of Iowa

When the University of Iowa (UI) Libraries launched its first crowdsourcing initiative in the spring of 2011, staff members weren't sure what kind of response to expect. The Civil War Diaries and Letters Transcription Project was planned as an experiment, an add-on at the end of a two-year manuscript-scanning effort to mark the Civil War sesquicentennial; the goal was to promote the digital collection by inviting the public to view handwritten documents online and type in the text to make it machine searchable. Lacking the major grant funds and teams of expert programmers that other institutions were investing in transcription crowdsourcing projects, we were able to pull together a solution by largely bypassing technical infrastructure in favor of e-mailed submissions, a lot of cutting and pasting, and blind enthusiasm.

A year after launch, the success of the project had surpassed everyone's expectations. The public had tirelessly transcribed the entire Civil War collection of 15,000 pages, the library received a steady stream of media attention about the initiative, and donors drawn to the site were gifting family diaries and letters to our special collections department. For digital library staff, however, enthusiasm was waning as the project's inefficiencies increasingly took its toll.

The completion of our initial offering of manuscripts provided an opportunity to take a step back, evaluate the project, and try to build on its success while addressing some of its problems. The end result, DIY

History (http://diyhistory.lib.uiowa.edu), was launched in October 2012, powered by streamlined scanning workflows, new strategies for increasing user engagement, and the introduction of infrastructure courtesy of Scripto, an open-source tool for crowdsourcing documentary transcription (see figure 11.1).

This is the story of how the UI Libraries expanded its early experiments with crowdsourcing to develop a scalable and sustainable public engagement program.

PLANNING

First, a note about why we decided to pursue crowdsourcing as a sanctioned library program: Yes, we have an inexhaustible need to make our digital collections more accessible on the web. Many scanned documents are handwritten and aren't full-text searchable without costly transcription work, and photographs often lack descriptive information that allows users to access them through a word search, such as many people want to do using tools like Google. For many organizations, enlisting free help from the public to transcribe and describe these digitized artifacts has proved a smart method to begin tackling the issue. But a funny thing happened on the way to our goal of enhancing the collections for theoretical end users (i.e., scholars who might use the transcriptions in their research): We ended up creating crowds of actual end users deeply en-

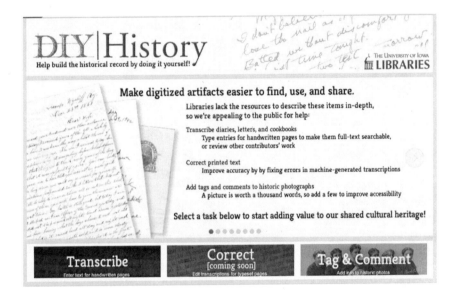

Figure 11.1.   The more thoughtfully designed DIY History site (http://diyhistory.lib.uiowa.edu) debuted in fall 2012.

gaged in meaningful interactions with the materials. In one of many insightful posts on the subject, digital archivist and blogger Trevor Owens describes this as the "upside-down objective" approach to crowdsourcing projects:

> Getting transcriptions, or for that matter getting any kind of data or work is a by-product of something that is actually far more amazing than being able to better search through a collection. The process of crowdsourcing projects fulfills the mission of digital collections better than the resulting searches. That is, when someone sits down to transcribe a document they are actually better fulfilling the mission of the cultural heritage organization than anyone who simply stops by to flip through the pages.[1]

With the Civil War project, we heard from many volunteers who developed a personal connection to the letters and diaries; from those who told us they only meant to transcribe a few pages but kept going after becoming invested in the story; to our most powerful of power users who, after completing 1,800 pages on his own, said the original writers felt like family. These connections with users and their sustained interest in the collections convinced us that we wanted to make a long-term commitment to engaging the public with a meaningful way to contribute to sustaining our shared cultural heritage.

The original site allowed transcribers to advance through the series of diaries and letters to experience a compelling narrative-driven story of a life during the Civil War (see figure 11.2). Page images drawn from CONTENTdm, our digital library content management system (CMS), were paired with a text box where users could type in transcriptions, hit "Submit," and advance to the next page. Behind the scenes, submitted transcripts would arrive in our departmental inbox, where cataloging staff would proof them, paste them into CONTENTdm, and index the collection. It was only then that a transcription became live and searchable.

Two main factors contributed to the site's success: content and simplicity. The transcription project was an afterthought to the digital collection, but even if we had planned it from the beginning, we could hardly have chosen better than Civil War materials. One look at a nonfiction bestseller list (or recent Oscar nominations) shows that the era is endlessly fascinating to Americans. A collection strength of UI's holdings, our Civil War correspondents and diarists range from high-ranking officers to foot soldiers on the front lines, society women volunteering at hospitals, and farm wives struggling to run households on their own. Actively helping many voices tell different parts of the same story let our transcribers make real-world connections to the past via the drama of battle, the tedium of life at camp, and the emotional pain of separation from loved ones. While developing the site to enable these connections, our aim was to make it simple and easy to use and keep the barriers to participation

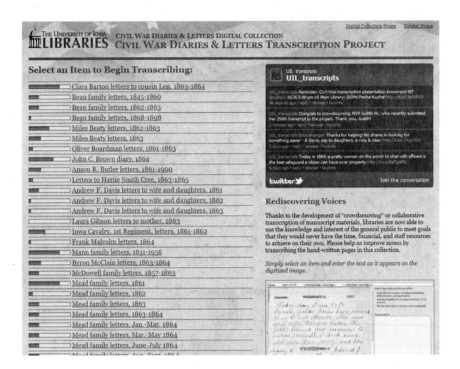

Figure 11.2. The experimental Civil War Diaries and Letters Transcription Project was launched in spring 2011 and retired in summer 2012.

low. No log-in was required, and users could start transcribing immediately, just one click off the home page.

Yet the simplicity of the site had its drawbacks. There was no way for the public to edit transcriptions or communicate to us, except via e-mail, let alone communicate with other transcribers. The asynchronous nature of the update process led to occasional duplicate submissions, and the mediation and manual labor required by staff ran counter to the spirit of a project aimed at leveraging technology and trusting the crowd. We knew, if we were going to move this project into a supported program of the libraries, we would need to make the process more efficient for staff and more interactive for the user.

Our goal for the new site was to create a scalable platform that would allow the public to help us make more accessible a variety of special collections materials. With the Civil War papers mostly complete, we hoped to retain our current volunteers while attracting new users by adding collections with different formats and content. While digital library staff investigated software options for the site expansion, curators worked on materials selection so that our preservation department could kick into high gear, amassing large quantities of digitized content to await the crowds upon relaunch.

A review of materials meeting our selection criteria—handwritten, historic value, high volume, requiring transcription to be truly useful— led to the choice of the first major collection to promote on the new site: the Szathmary culinary manuscripts. Dating from the seventeenth century to the early 1960s, these handwritten cookbooks contain thousands of pages detailing recipes for oddities like "pickilled cowcumbers," calves feet jelly, spiced tongue, and dandelion wine. Along with specialist users like cultural historians and foodies, we hoped the novelty of the manuscripts would translate to crossover appeal for a more general audience. Additionally, the new site would feature smaller collections of letters and diaries, including materials from the Iowa Women's Archives as well as new acquisitions of Civil War items.

Selecting software to power the site expansion was fairly straightforward. Scripto, an open-source tool for collaborative manuscript transcription that had only recently received National Endowment for the Humanities (NEH) development funding when we first researched options for the Civil War site, was now fully launched and ready for download. Created by George Mason University, Scripto works in tandem with existing content management systems, such as Omeka, WordPress, and Drupal, integrating transcription capture into digital library infrastructure, which would solve our manual processing lag time and duplicate submission problems. Its wiki technology lets users not only create transcriptions but also edit existing ones—a vast improvement over our current workflow, with users e-mailing lengthy lists of corrections and library staff tracking the pages down in CONTENTdm to make the edits one by one. Even better, the wiki features allow staff to elevate power users to deputies who can help monitor and oversee submissions. Much like Wikipedia's model of granting editor status to proven contributors, this approach would crowdsource some of the project's workflow duties back to the volunteers, creating a more scalable approach to managing submissions. Having found a match to our technological enhancement wish list, our IT staff set to work getting Scripto up and running.

Giving users the power to proofread represented a philosophical as well as a technological shift in our workflows. The success of the Civil War project provided ample evidence of return on investment (ROI)—the anticipated amount of benefit generated as a direct result of an expenditure—to convince administrators that this project was worth developing. But to make a crowdsourcing program sustainable, we needed to find ways to put bounds around staff time. Mediation of individual transcriptions—the necessity of moving submissions from e-mail to the content management system—provided an opportunity to check for typos or attempt to fill in missed words. This aided in quality assurance, but the practice didn't scale at the rate transcriptions were arriving. In the end, we decided that, for the sake of sustainability and the spirit of the project, we needed to move away from any attempts to proofread the submissions and grow our tolerance for imperfection. If we were asking the crowd for help, we needed to put our trust in them.

In addition to copying, pasting, and proofreading, another ineffective use of scarce staff resources that we needed to address was the amount of time spent answering e-mails. Responsiveness to users is an essential part of crowdsourcing efforts, but the way we were doing it, one on one and offline, felt inefficient. We also wanted to provide a space where our transcribers could communicate among themselves and develop a sense of community. To this end, we created a discussion forum for the site where staff could answer questions and post news and volunteers could chat with each other about the project.

Last but not least, we needed a new name for the site. The decidedly unwieldy *Civil War Diaries and Letters Transcription Project* lacked the scalability as well as the catchiness of other crowdsourcing initiatives, such as NARA's recently launched *Citizen Archivist* site. In his article "Crowdsourcing the Humanities: Social Research and Collaboration," Geoffrey Rockwell calls this the "high concept, good title" rule of successful crowdsourcing projects:

> For volunteers to decide to participate in a crowdsourcing project, they need to understand what they are committing to. It is important, therefore, to communicate efficiently the idea of the project. A title for a project like "Wikipedia" goes a long way towards describing the project—that is, it is an encyclopedia created with a wiki.[2]

Like a miniature elevator speech, the title should attempt to convey the point of the site. At the same time, we wanted to avoid the shortcut of including the word *crowdsourcing*, which can have negative connotations, according to Owens:

> Both the idea of the crowd and the notion of sourcing are terrible terms for folks working as stewards for our cultural heritage. Many of the projects that end up falling under the heading of crowdsourcing in libraries, archives and museums have not involved large and massive crowds and they have very little to do with outsourcing labor.[3]

Rather than faceless masses doing menial tasks, he argues, our volunteers are interested members of the public engaging in meaningful work.

With these criteria in mind, we decided to align ourselves with the do-it-yourself movement in home repair, crafting, and punk rock—that is, creating something without the aid of professionals—by selecting the name *DIY History*.

IMPLEMENTATION

This time around we wouldn't have the luxury of spending two years on scanning to create a large and comprehensive digital collection the way we did with the Civil War materials. Planning for DIY History began in earnest during the late spring of 2012, with a target date of early fall, leaving just a few months for our preservation staff to make their way through one of the most challenging reformatting projects they had ever faced. While the Civil War collections were fairly uniform—dating from roughly the same time period, comprising mostly loose correspondence or small diaries designed to be carried in soldiers' pockets—the manuscript cookbooks were anything but. Spanning several centuries and varying widely in length, size, paper and ink type, page attachment, and binding, they required a variety of conservation treatments and had to be reformatted exclusively on our lone top-down scanner. We were forced to reexamine long-held procedures for scanning, with an eye toward streamlining. One instance involved rethinking our time-consuming image editing tasks. Usually handmade and not at all uniform, the cookbooks often had different-sized pages that were crooked in real life.

Recognizing that the attempt to impose uniformity through digital means where it didn't exist in real life was contrary to the nature of the materials, so we made the decision to forego image editing altogether. The resulting scans were not only much quicker to produce, but they also gave users a better sense of the physical items in all their imperfections.

Another reformatting step in need of rethinking was the scanning of all pages of a book, front and back, including blanks. Digital library staff had long considered this a less-than-user-friendly practice resulting in digital objects that required many extra clicks of the mouse for users to get to the desired information. Preservation staff, with a predigitization history of reformatting for microform, argued for the continued importance of creating master image files that were exact facsimiles of the physical objects. However, new staff bringing a fresh eye to the workflows—in the face of sometimes massive cookbooks that might contain several hundred blank pages—brought about a reconsideration, and that practice was abandoned.

While preservation ramped up scanning production, our IT staff were having mixed results with the implementation of Scripto. As mentioned, it's a tool to use in conjunction with some content management systems, but unfortunately CONTENTdm, which powers our digital library, isn't one of them. Instead we installed Scripto along with Omeka, the open-source CMS designed for use by scholars to create digital collections and exhibits (both tools were developed at George Mason University's Center for History and New Media). Installation was fairly straightforward, but as we prepared to start exporting image files and metadata from CONTENTdm, we hit a snag with Omeka's batch import tool. Designed only to import metadata at the item level—that is, the description of the cookbook as a whole—we were losing important page-level data, such as page numbers and existing transcripts. Once our technology team fixed this by customizing the batch import tool to harvest both data types—along the way, making the code available online for the benefit of other Omeka users—support staff got to work moving thousands of pages of digitized manuscripts from one system to the other.

Further customizations included the creation of a new theme because the software's out-of-the-box presentation and navigation didn't totally suit our needs. Following Omeka's primary function as an exhibit tool, the existing themes focused too heavily on displaying digitized artifacts, with transcription functionality as an accessory. Because we already have a digital library site for users interested in browsing and searching our collections, we weren't interested in duplicating these features at DIY History. Shifting the focus, our IT staff designed Scribe, a minimalist theme that strips out much of the software's navigation and exhibition functionality in order to put transcription collection front and center. Along with the rest of our customizations, the Scribe code has been made available at DIY History for other institutions to use.

Another problem requiring a significant investment in programming time was addressing Scripto's lack of status or progress display functionality. Without this feature users couldn't identify from the browse screen which items were nearly completed and which hadn't been started; instead, they had to click through to the page level and view whether there was any text present in the transcription box. In addition to lacking user-friendliness in terms of navigation, this is also contrary to best practices recommending a visual display to show users the effect they're having on project goals. In her seminal article on library crowdsourcing, Rose Holley explains the importance of this practice, quoting a successful project manager:

> "Any time that you're trying to get people to give you stuff, to do stuff for you, the most important thing is that people know that what they're doing is having an effect. It's kind of a fundamental tenet of social software. . . . If you're not giving people the 'I rock' vibe, you're not getting people to stick around." You must let volunteers know how well they are doing to keep their motivation up. [4]

Once our IT staff developed a solution for creating item-level progress bars, we used it as our default sorting criteria on transcription collection home pages, so that items needing the most work were displayed at the top of the page, with completed items down at the bottom. [5]

The final major issue we wrestled with involved transcription workflow and the role of deputies. We knew that we wanted to give our power users an expanded role in reviewing and editing duties, but we weren't sure exactly how that role would look. As in many stages of the redesign process, working from our past model for the Civil War project proved to be both a blessing and a curse. It provided a head start, so we weren't designing tasks from scratch, but as we quickly realized, sometimes previous procedures no longer made sense in the new environment.

In the past a paraprofessional staff member and a student assistant pasted user-submitted transcriptions from e-mail messages into CONTENTdm; over time, for better or worse, this manual migration task grew to include proofing and revising the data as well. A main factor in this workflow was the asynchronous nature of the submission process; because the transcription web form was dynamically generated from images and data in CONTENTdm, a transcribed page appeared to be blank until staff pasted in the user submission. This placed a strong emphasis on processing materials—that is, moving them to the "done" pile—quickly.

With Scripto, any user can create or edit transcriptions. Those with elevated status, such as library staff or deputized power users, can mark records as final and lock them down from further editing, at which point they would be moved to the digital library to comprise a permanent part of our metadata records. Because the transcriptions would now show up on DIY History immediately thanks to Scripto, there wasn't the same urgency in finalizing records so as to avoid duplicate submissions that we experienced with the Civil War site. Once we realized that, we began to question the need to finalize records at all. At this stage, project meetings sometimes ground to a halt as discussion took an accidental turn to the existential: What does it mean to approve? What is "done"?

It turns out we were stumbling upon another crowdsourcing best practice described by Rockwell as the "knowledge in process" rule:

> Like many digital projects, crowdsourcing projects should be thought of as processes not products. Articles in the Wikipedia are continually being edited—often, but not always, for the better. If you see an error, fix it. Crowdsourced knowledge is therefore more of a relationship than a finished object. It starts out tentative and then slowly gets refined. The history of that process is often available, which adds an open dimension to the knowledge in process. With Wikipedia articles, you can see their editing history and unwind it.[6]

For our project a breakthrough came when we learned of CONTENTdm Catcher, a web-based tool that does allow batch overlays of data in CONTENTdm, leaving reference URLs intact. With this new information, we happily canceled plans to perform manual data migration, instead opting for regularly scheduled automated updates of transcriptions to the digital library, regardless of their status (not started, in progress, needing review, or approved). Elevated users would still have approval powers at

DIY History, but digital library users wouldn't have to wait for this approval before accessing the transcriptions in process.

We cultivated relationships with a handful of power users, some of whom got in touch with us with questions and comments. Others who voluntarily provided their e-mail addresses were targeted with an e-mail solicitation to help us improve the user experience. The first use of our power users was in the role of beta testers prior to launch. Their feedback was encouraging; aside from a few minor bugs and suggestions for rewording instructional text, reactions were mostly positive. Overall, the testers found the site easy to use, giving high praise to the simplicity of the interface and to the addition of more options, contentwise.

Regardless, library staff were still apprehensive going into launch. The site worked fine with a handful of people using it, but could it withstand the stress of crowds of users? Worse yet, what if there were too few users—would we lose our old audience and fail to attract a new one? The Civil War materials had been so successful, and we weren't sure how a launch based around the historic cookbooks would compare. Would people keep coming back without the narrative hook provided by diaries and letters? At last, after several postponements and an official launch date that gave way to a soft launch, we held our collective breath and sent out a press release in early October, announcing DIY History to the world.

RESULTS

Early usage of the site was brisk, with respectable but not server-crashing usage statistics (4,400 visitors and 45,000 page views in the first month after launch). This was bolstered by press coverage from local media outlets, following up on previous stories about our Civil War site. Twitter was also driving much of the traffic, with links to DIY History reaching upward of 40,000 accounts, according to statistics at the analytics site TweetReach. But as with our previous launch, it was a social link-sharing site that made the biggest impact, PR-wise. Instead of Reddit, which helped put Civil War transcription on the map, this time around it was Metafilter that got us the most attention—both from potential volunteers and from the mainstream media.

In a post titled "Want to Make Historic Recipes?" a Metafilter user going by the name "cashman" linked to DIY History, providing a couple of sample recipes: pecan balls from a 1948 Girl Scouts cookbook, as well as a "sure cure for black diphtheria" from 1880. Soon the commenters were off and running, posting recipe links, transcription advice, and, gratifyingly, positive reactions to the site:

> Good lord, I could do this all day. It is so much fun to look at this stuff and a great help for everyone.

Now this is the way to crowdsource transcription work. The last time I saw one of these here, there were intricate instructions and varying sign-up processes . . . and a month later, I've still not gotten a login. This one is much easier.

Heck, I just finished 3 recipes from the 1933 cookbook. I'm not sure why I find this to be fun, but I do.

Fabulous! I love old cookbooks and getting access to non-published ones is great. What a wonderful project.

Ooooooh. This is fun! I suppose I define "fun" in a less-than-traditional way.[7]

Our stats after this post spiked to more than 2,100 visitors and 21,000 page views in a single day. National and even international news outlets picked up the story from there, most notably Eatocracy, CNN's food blog, and *Wired UK*'s blog.

After this mini rush, visitors to the site dropped off to a smaller but steady user group, as is typical for crowdsourcing projects, averaging around 1,000 visitors and 20,000 page views per month. This phenomenon is addressed in two more tips from Rockwell—"support imbalance" and "small crowds work too":

An imbalance between contributors is normal, so you should plan for it. A small number of participants will contribute a lot each, while a large number will contribute a little. . . . The success of a crowdsourcing project need not depend on large numbers of contributors. The numbers of collaborators [may be] small, especially when compared to large-scale projects like the Wikipedia, but the numbers [are] sufficient to achieve progress.[8]

Small but steady is definitely winning the race at our redesigned site; while the initial offering of 15,000 Civil War pages were transcribed in a year and a half, our DIY History users completed the same amount of transcriptions in a little more than three months.

LESSONS LEARNED

While we're very pleased with the overall success of the redesign, there are a few aspects that didn't quite work out and are thus being dropped from the site. Early on in the reformatting process, it became apparent that many of our manuscript items—especially the twentieth-century cookbooks and sets of correspondence—contained typeset text among the handwritten pages. We were able to create machine-generated transcriptions by using optical character recognition (OCR) technology on these typewritten letters and pasted-in newspaper clippings, but they were often in need of substantial cleanup—much more so than the manually created submissions. After migrating the OCR'd transcriptions to DIY History along with the rest of the CONTENTdm data, we hoped to interest volunteers in proofreading them as a separate task option on our home page. However, there wasn't a simple solution in Scripto for isolating just the typeset pages, so we couldn't provide a link to only those items. Next, we briefly considered developing plans for a separate historic newspaper OCR cleanup project for the site, following the example of such massively successful initiatives as the National Library of Australia's Trove effort.[9] Ultimately, however, the main reason we rejected the newspaper idea was due to rapid advancements in OCR technology. With the accuracy of machine-generated transcriptions improving all the time, we thought it best to anticipate redoing OCR scanning of typeset documents down the road, while focusing current crowdsourcing efforts exclusively on handwritten manuscripts.

One alternate task that we did get to work—functionally, at least— was an option from the DIY History home page for users to tag and comment on historic photos at the UI Libraries Flickr site. Inspired by the phenomenal success of the Library of Congress and other institutions participating in the Flickr Commons initiative, we migrated some of our own content to the photo-sharing site to try to get our images "in the flow"—that is, push it to where the users are rather than try to pull the users to us. While we are very pleased with the usage statistics—page views on Flickr are exponentially higher compared to the same content in our digital library—the vast majority of users are viewing, favoriting, and adding our images to groups, with commenting happening rarely and tagging almost never. After considering such options as more aggressive promotion or switching out some of the content, we eventually decided to leave the photos in Flickr but drop that component as part of DIY History and return to a focus on transcription only.

Finally, we've recently decided to discontinue the DIY History discussion forum. Although a few transcribers have used it to ask questions and report problems, the posts primarily ended up to be staff members talking to other staff members. As with all social media, discussion forums are free but also costly in terms of time spent seeding it with content and trying to promote its use. This lack of user participation aligns with findings by the University College London's *Transcribe Bentham* team, who conducted user studies for their transcription crowdsourcing project. While they anticipated that their otherwise highly engaged volunteers would communicate with each other on the site's discussion forum, this participation never materialized. Responses to user surveys indicated that "volunteers appeared to prefer . . . to work alone, with communication and acknowledgement from staff being of much greater importance than collaboration with other users."[10]

On the plus side, our apprehension about the cookbooks and their lack of narrative proved to be groundless, as we've had no problem attracting users to this content. Plans are currently underway to expand the site's manuscript offerings even further, with the library embarking on major scanning initiatives for pioneer-era letters and diaries, as well as those related to World War II. On the technology front, transition to Omeka and Scripto has been relatively smooth once we completed the initial implementation, liberating our library assistants from their cut-and-paste duties. Our developers are building on this success with a project to create a new open-source tool, one that will allow crowdsourcing for semantic markup of transcriptions. When it's finished, volunteers will be able to structure the texts by adding tags for places, dates, and recipe elements, such as ingredients or measurements.

CONCLUSION

Such tweaks to the site, both major and minor, have become part of a continuous redesign as the project grows and evolves. While content and technology may change, our commitment to the core of library crowd-sourcing initiatives—engaging users and adding value to collections—stays constant.

This experiment has evolved into a programmatic effort at the librar-ies as the value of cultivating participatory archives—contributions to enhance the value and utility of archival materials by a broad public—becomes fully realized. This work has not only cultivated an engaged user base, but it has also led to additional donations that have allowed us to expand our holdings. Moreover, the project has caused us to rethink priorities in every aspect of our activities, from acquisitions to digitiza-tion selection to promotion and outreach. While our bibliographers scour eBay for manuscript cookbooks and other handwritten materials for the site, digital library staff are investigating possibilities for crowdsourcing selection for all digitization efforts, not just those for DIY History, and our special collections outreach librarian invites users on social media to pick the focus of her rare books video series on YouTube. With the grow-ing awareness of just how scarce our resources are, library staff can use crowdsourcing to pinpoint efforts on what users really want, helping to take some of the guesswork out of serving the public.

Creating a transcription project to achieve these goals is now easier than ever. Our advice is to start small, choose content wisely, and don't be afraid of experimenting with low-tech solutions because early success on the cheap can help you build the case for more resources. With crowd-sourcing still a relatively recent phenomenon, none of us are experts in this area; a do-it-yourself approach to building these projects can pay off big for your users and your institution.

Jen Wolfe is digital scholarship librarian, digital research and publishing, at the University of Iowa Libraries. *Nicole Saylor* is the head of the archive at the American Folklife Center, Library of Congress. Until November 2012, she was the head, digital research and publishing, at the University of Iowa Libraries.

NOTES

1. Trevor Owens, "Crowdsourcing Cultural Heritage: The Objectives Are Upside Down," *Trevor Owens: User Centered Digital History* (blog), March 10, 2012, http://www.trevorowens.org/2012/03/crowdsourcing-cultural-heritage-the-objectives-are-upside-down.

2. Geoffrey Rockwell, "Crowdsourcing the Humanities: Social Research and Collaboration," in *Collaborative Research in the Digital Humanities* , ed. Marilyn Deegan and Willard McCarty (Farnham, Surrey, Great Britain: Ashgate, 2010), 135–54.

3. Trevor Owens, "The Crowd and the Library," *Trevor Owens: User Centered Digital History* (blog), May 20, 2012, http://www.trevorowens.org/2012/05/the-crowd-and-the-library.

4. Rose Holley, "Crowdsourcing: How and Why Should Libraries Do It?" *D-Lib Magazine* 16, nos. 3–4 (2010), accessed May 4, 2013, http://www.dlib.org/dlib/march10/holley/03holley.html.

5. For more information about the technical implementation of Scripto, see Shawn Averkamp and Matthew Butler, "The Care and Feeding of a Crowd" (presentation at Code4Lib Conference, Chicago, Illinois, February 14, 2013), http://ir.uiowa.edu/lib_pubs/129.

6. Rockwell, "Crowdsourcing the Humanities," 149.

7. "cashman," "Want to Make Historic Recipes?" Metafilter, October 27, 2012, http://www.metafilter.com/121316/Want-to-Make-Historic-Recipes.

8. Rockwell, 147.

9. "Trove," *National Library of Australia*, accessed September 15, 2013, http://trove.nla.gov.au.

10. Tim Causer and Valerie Wallace, "Building a Volunteer Community: Results and Findings from *Transcribe Bentham*," *Digital Humanities Quarterly* 6, no. 2 (2012) http://www.digitalhumanities.org/dhq/vol/6/2/000125/000125.html.

TWELVE

Taking Preservation to the People

Educating the Public about Personal Digital Archiving

William LeFurgy, Library of Congress

As manager of the Library of Congress's National Digital Information Infrastructure and Preservation Program (NDIIPP), I'm responsible for implementing a national strategy to collect, preserve, and make available significant digital content for current and future generations. Much of this work has focused on collaborations with large cultural heritage institutions. These projects typically involve working with experts to address complex technological and social challenges related to managing large digital collections over time. But we are concerned as well with cultural heritage institutions of all sizes that manage, or wish to manage, digital content. We promote sharing of the latest tools, practices, and learning of value to the broad population of librarians and archivists.

The NDIIPP scope also reaches beyond collecting institutions to the millions of individuals and families who have built collections of personal digital materials. These personal items are at very high risk of loss due to changing technology, unreliable storage media, and the biggest problem of all: lack of public awareness about the need to manage their content. We at the Library of Congress are committed, through public outreach and engagement, to help people and their families have enduring access to their digital memories.

This is a compelling issue. We live in an age where millions of people have quickly amassed large digital collections of family photographs and videos, as well as e-mail and social media postings. These digital items have largely replaced such traditional analog media as photo albums, letters, and film-based home movies. In addition, the expectation among many is that ongoing digital access to current information—as well as to older hard-copy materials—is required. This change closely follows the stunningly rapid spread of digital technology into people's lives. Twenty years ago the Internet was a novelty for a few hard-core enthusiasts. The same was true of computers, digital cameras, and mobile phones. Ten years ago Flickr, YouTube, and Facebook did not exist. And the rate of technological change and its impact on how we record our lives will certainly continue.

I know from personal, as well as professional, experience that the ease by which digital materials are created and shared obscures a troubling fact: Managing, preserving, and ensuring continuing access to digital objects is difficult. Unlike traditional photographic prints or paper letters, digital files are intangible. They depend entirely on machines to find and use them. These machines change rapidly; laptops, mobile phones, and entirely new devices come and go every few years. We don't even see many of the virtual cloud-based machines we depend on to store files. A result is that personal files are scattered among different devices, local and remote. The potential for losing files is great when these devices fail or are replaced. Risk rises with the degree to which files are spread among devices, both in terms of the probability of loss and the chance that people will simply lose track of the content.

Traditional family photos and other information sources are relatively durable and low maintenance. Family albums can easily be stored on a shelf for decades with very little discernible degradation. But computer files depend on changing technology: The software used to read the files changes, as does the type of machine available to view them. The biggest problem is the short life span of the physical media used to store the files. Currently there is no truly "archival" media. Hard disks, flash drives, CDs, DVDs—none of them are intended for long-term storage. All of them will eventually fail and lose data. Reputable cloud storage services are a bit more reliable in the short term, but as commercial entities, their long-term existence is uncertain.

Another question is also lurking in the background: How successfully can we pass on our personal digital collections? We likely have some idea where our files are and know something about their provenance and context, but an inheritor may only see an undifferentiated digital mess— that is, if they are even able to find and access the files in the first place. As time passes the prospect of enormous loss of family and community heritage grows ever larger.

At the Library of Congress, we worry that the rise of digital technology also imperils traditional family memory resources. Many people are rushing to create digital copies of photographic prints and slides, for example. The motivation for this is fine: a desire for enhanced sharing of and access to the content. But careless handling may damage original items, and they may even be lost if they have to be sent away for processing. An even greater threat may be loss of interest in the originals once they are scanned or converted. With the ever-growing focus on the digital, analog originals may be neglected or even discarded.

All of these factors led us to launch a personal digital archiving outreach initiative with two audiences in mind. One is the general public, and with this in mind, we designed an array of resources along with a number of delivery and communication methods. The second audience is librarians and archivists who might wish to undertake their own institutional outreach programs. For this purpose we packaged resources along with ideas and guidance for different kinds of outreach strategies.

This chapter is specifically about how we developed resources, events, and activities for the first audience. Let me say, however, that I feel strongly that the skills of librarians and archivists are well suited to help the millions of people now struggling to manage their unruly digital collections. I believe that institutions of all sizes now have a great opportunity to bring innovative services to their communities through outreach targeting this issue. In addition to helping ordinary people preserve a personal legacy, this work also can lend itself well to inviting patrons to donate digital items that document community history. Local digital heritage collections strengthen community identity, support lifelong learning, and demonstrate a new and compelling relevance for libraries and other collecting institutions.

The question sometimes arises about why we use the phrase *personal digital archiving*. As a trained archivist, I long resisted use of this proud noun as a verb. But ultimately I concluded it was a futile struggle. *Archiving* as a verb simply has acquired too much momentum in modern English to resist with any hope of success. Jumping from widespread use in enterprise storage and information technology environments, *archiving* now commonly is used to mean moving digital information to centralized, relatively secure storage for some period of time, or "to file or collect in or as if in an archive."[1] We figured that *archiving* would resonate more with the general public than would *preservation* or another word. (It also sounds better in gerund form; *personal digital preserving* doesn't really work.) We can't even claim to have coined the phrase. Catherine C. Marshall was using it as early as 2006, for example.[2]

PLANNING

In 2009, we noticed there was a shortage of accessible guidance and advice for personal digital archiving. The digital preservation policies, standards, and best practices designed for trained professionals are too dense and complex for most ordinary people to use. Where they existed, resources aimed at the general public were often obscure and hard to find.

We heard quite a bit about the advantages of digital technology and the desirability of the newest devices, but warnings about the risks to personal digital collections were typically few and faint. As a result, we found through interviews with Library of Congress visitors, as well as through anecdotal research, that people in general were not aware of the risk to their personal digital materials. Perhaps this is because computers encourage a casual approach to creation and management; it's quite easy to assume all those unseen files are safe—until a hard drive fails, a smartphone is lost, or an Internet service goes away.

Given our mission, we defined a very broad audience for our public archiving outreach. We wanted to cover the most common types of content, and we wanted to deliver our message through a number of different events and communication channels. Early in our planning process, we also decided that we wanted to base our guidance on a foundation of professional practice while also ensuring that it was as easy as possible for a nonspecialist to understand and act upon. As noted, there was little in the way of existing models to guide our work; that meant we had to plan for drafting our guidance from scratch.

At the start of our planning, we focused exclusively on material already in digital form, either born-digital or digital copies of analog items. We purposefully stayed away from anything relating to the digitization process, as it is typically not a preservation activity in itself. But, as noted later, many lay people simply assume that digital preservation and digital archiving are inextricably related to scanning hard-copy originals. This association is so strong, in fact, that we subsequently planned separate guidance for digitization, being sure to urge proper care of the resulting digital copies.

We moved on to define the categories of digital content that our guidance was to cover. From discussions among staff and with external individuals, we determined that we would focus on broad information categories that people could readily identify with and that likely appeared with the highest frequency in personal collections:

- Photographs
- Audio
- Video
- Electronic Mail
- Personal Digital Documents
- Websites

The last two categories are purposefully general. *Personal digital documents* was meant to cover word-processing files, spreadsheets, and other items—separate from the above—generated by desktop software applications. *Websites* covers traditional web pages as well as social media streams from Facebook, Twitter, and other platforms. It is certainly arguable that both categories could be split into multiple separate groupings, but we determined that a higher-level classification would allow us to cover a broader scope with fewer words. It is also worth noting that certain kinds of digital content, including text messages, 3D design models, and software (including video games), are not covered. In some cases, personal-level guidance may exist for excluded content categories, but an institution interested in outreach for them likely will need to draft something new.

The next step in our planning was arguably the hardest: figuring out how to distill professional digital preservation practice down to basic actions that ordinary people can effectively understand and implement. We came up with four activities: identify (analogous to inventory), decide (appraise), organize (arrange and describe), and make copies (sustain and preserve). These actions are meant to provide a basic framework of tips for people to use as a way to get started managing their personal collections. No attempt was made to be comprehensive; the idea is that, once people get started, they can seek out more in-depth guidance. We wanted to present a low bar to getting started, as we believed that many people are easily intimidated by technical instruction as well as reluctant to undertake a project that demands too much time. While following each of the steps sequentially is ideal, they are also designed to accommodate even limited, irregular efforts to improve collection management. This guidance is obviously too simple to yield consistent professional results, but we felt that increasing usability and reducing the risk of loss for personal collections were the preferred outcomes.

We sought to adapt these four actions to suit the six content types identified earlier. As an example, here are the activities outlined for personal digital photographs on the NDIIPP personal digital archiving web page (see Textbox 12.1).[3]

When we completed our narrative guidance, which took about three months, we moved on to implementation planning. As noted, our original intent was to use a variety of events and information delivery methods to get our message out. In terms of events, we intended to participate in high-profile Library of Congress public events that were already scheduled. Our initial planning was concurrent with the first "National Preservation Week (NPW)," sponsored by the American Library Association and others; we determined that we would follow the advice of NPW organizers and hold dedicated "Personal Archiving Day" events to interact with individuals. We also decided that we would seek collaborations with other cultural heritage organizations—large and small—to participate in public outreach events. Our planning also fortunately coincided with the commencement of official NDIIPP social media accounts, including Facebook and Twitter. Use of those channels to communicate— and ideally engage—with people was a central part of our outreach strategy from the start.

1. Identify where you have digital photos
   a. Identify all your digital photos on cameras, computers, and removable media, such as memory cards.
   b. Include your photos on the web.

2. Decide which photos are most important
   a. Pick the images you feel are especially important.
   b. You can pick a few photos or many.
   c. If there are multiple versions of an important photo, save the one with highest quality.

3. Organize the selected photos
   a. Give individual photos descriptive file names.
   b. Tag photos with names of people and descriptive subjects.
   c. Create a directory/folder structure on your computer to put the images you picked.
   d. Write a brief description of the directory structure and the photos.

4. Make copies and store them in different places
   a. Make at least two copies of your selected photos—more copies are better.
   b. One copy can stay on your computer or laptop; put other copies on separate media, such as DVDs, CDs, portable hard drives, thumb drives, or Internet storage.
   c. Store copies in different locations that are as physically far apart as practical. If disaster strikes one location, your photographs in the other place should be safe.
   d. Put a copy of the photo inventory with your important papers in a secure location.
   e. Check your photos at least once a year to make sure you can read them.
   f. Create new media copies every five years or when necessary to avoid data loss.

Textbox 12.1. Example of the kinds of activities outlined on the NDIIPP personal digital archiving website

IMPLEMENTATION

Given our ambitious intent, implementation of our personal digital archiving outreach rolled out over the course of several months. We used a two-track approach: "virtual" by means of the Internet and "in person" through public events. Our first action was to publish the narrative guidance noted earlier on our website. On the advice of professional web designers, we deployed the information via a graphically rich subsection of the website with succinct text. The new section, "Personal Archiving: Preserving Your Digital Memories,"[4] immediately became one of the website's most popular destinations, receiving many thousands of page views in a short time.

There is no doubt that the large majority of people who came across our personal archiving guidance did so via the Internet. A key element of our strategy was to leverage links from other web pages. We notified related institutions and organizations about our resources with some success. The American Library Association's (ALA) Public Library Association listed our guidance as a digital literacy resource.[5] The ALA website for National Preservation Week also linked to our website,[6] as does the Association of College and Research Libraries,[7] Kansas State Historical Society,[8] and — crucially, because it drives lots of traffic — Wikipedia.[9]

All of our subsequent efforts built on the information we placed on the web. These efforts took place in parallel. After the web section launched, for example, we began producing a series of personal archiving videos. We did our best to meet the basic requirements for video on the web: short, amusing, and full of interesting visual content. The videos are specifically intended to build awareness by appealing to audiences who may not necessarily be drawn to textual advice. Our titles include *Why Digital Preservation Is Important for You*, *Archiving Digital Photos*, and *Adding Descriptions to Digital Photos: Your Gift to the Future*. Each production touched on our basic guidance framework and also includes the website URL at the end. We placed the videos on our Library of Congress website, as well as on YouTube.[10]

We also created a series of leaflets dealing with specific personal archiving topics, including *How to Scan Your Personal Collections*, *How Long Will Digital Storage Media Last?*, and *How to Transfer Photos from Your Camera to Your Computer*. These leaflets serve a dual purpose: Individuals can download them from the program website, and NDIIPP staff can also print them as handouts for outreach events.

We repackaged the information noted earlier into a unique resource designed to help libraries and archives of all sizes sponsor outreach activities: the "Personal Digital Archiving Day Kit."[11] This publication contains a host of material to assist with everything from event planning to evaluation. The kit also contains practical advice distilled from the library's own experience in hosting or supporting public events.

As noted, we planned early to rely on social media to get our message out and, ideally, change behavior. The library's digital preservation blog, *The Signal*,[12] has served as a significant platform. We have published scores of posts in connection with personal digital archiving, covering topics including metadata, preferred file formats, digital estate planning, and more. The blog also gives us the opportunity to share personal experiences with preserving—and losing—digital content. I like to think that this personal approach humanizes the subject and makes it more appealing and relevant. The blog also provides a highly effective means to engage with people. Since its launch in 2011, the blog has received many dozens of comments and questions from ordinary people interested in preserving digital materials. Individual blog posts also have been cited and republished elsewhere, which greatly expands the reach of the original message. Blog posts are written in a conversational tone and are intended to connect with issues that matter to ordinary people; posts also often ask questions and encourage readers to respond. We also take the concept of content repurposing seriously and published a free e-book of personal archiving blog posts, *Perspectives on Personal Digital Archiving*.[13]

The NDIIPP Facebook page serves as another effective platform for personal archiving outreach.[14] Many of the posts refer to our own products and activities, but we also cite the work of other institutions from around the world. I find the personal archiving posts are often among the most popular on our page. A recent post reporting an NPR story, "In the Digital Age, The Family Photo Album Fades Away,"[15] drew more than 2,200 views, 21 "likes," and 26 shares. Another post linking to "Personal Digital Archiving—We Need to Fix the Scale Problem"[16] in ZDNet generated more than 4,300 views, 78 "likes," and 25 shares. While this is fairly lightweight engagement, it does indicate community reach and interest. Facebook also has the great advantage of reaching a huge audience that self-identifies with a specific institution or topic.

Our Twitter account is another mode for outreach. We use it to push out a variety of information, including regular details relating to personal digital archiving.[17] As with the NDIIPP Facebook account, we use the NDIIPP Twitter account to communicate about our guidance and related products. And, again, tweets on this particular subject tend to be among the most popular, garnering many retweets, favorites, and responses. I find Twitter, with its enforced brevity, to be a very effective outreach vehicle for our purposes. I should also note that a key aspect of our outreach implementation involves cross-posting notices and information among all our social media accounts. For example, a published blog post is cited in a Facebook post and a tweet. This amplifies the message with minimum effort.

One final element of our virtual outreach implementation involved using webinars: online presentations that participants can view individually or in groups anywhere with an Internet connection. We held several webinars[18] starting in 2011 that were attended live by five hundred or more people. Each presentation was also recorded and posted to the web for ongoing access. The webinars were held in conjunction with National Preservation Week and included "Preserving Your Personal Digital Memories" and "Preserving Your Personal Digital Photographs." Earlier this year we presented "Hosting a Personal Digital Archiving Day Event" specifically designed to help other cultural heritage organizations implement their own outreach events.

Our in-person public events fell into two groupings: We hosted our own at the Library of Congress, and we collaborated with other organizations. For the events in our space, the process began with picking a date; for example, many of our events have been held during NPW. We chose to hold a personal archiving day during this time to support the national intent of NPW and also to capitalize on publicity from the American Library Association and other organizations. Our approach to personal archiving day was straightforward: Talk to as many people as possible about managing their digital content. We also aimed to distribute information in the form of specialized handouts, as well as through bookmarks, stickers, and other items (all featuring our webpage URL and how to connect with us via social media). We have used different configurations, but the basic approach is to set up one or more tables in a public spot, place our information on the table, and make staff available to greet people and talk about personal archiving. One very effective way to draw people to the table is to display old computer hardware and storage media. Floppy disks; paper punch cards; old video game systems; and thirty-year-old, thirty-pound "portable" computers are magnets for all ages. Older people are nostalgic about devices once so familiar but haven't been seen in years. Children are fascinated by things that, by tech standards, look amazingly primitive. Once drawn in, staff have the chance to talk about computer obsolescence and the need to actively manage personal files. We have experimented with using a laptop and large display screens to show online resources but have found that direct person-to-person interactions work best.

We have also held outreach events in conjunction with a very popular local happening, the National Book Festival. The festival draws many thousands of people, and many of them have talked with us about personal digital preservation. This kind of event is ideal, as it offers a huge audience—many of them families taking digital pictures—who are ripe for helpful advice about passing on personal legacies.

Our events also have included other forms of information sharing, including staff lectures tailored to such special topics as preserving digital photographs. We have also featured "film festivals" of our video productions, as well as those of others. Another approach has involved the NDIIPP staff partnering with the physical preservation staff at the Library of Congress to present a comprehensive approach to preserving family heritage. As noted earlier, we found that many people assume that *digital archiving* includes making digital copies of analog materials. As a result, we receive many questions along the lines of "I have a collection of photo prints. What's the best way to archive them on the computer?" Rather than try to work against this notion, we provide basic scanning guidance along with tips for managing the digital copies; if our physical preservation colleagues are present, we encourage questioners to talk with them about caring for the analog originals.

Our collaborative events have been varied. We have partnered with the Smithsonian National Museum of African American History and Culture as part of their national road show, Save Our African American Treasures. In this case, personal digital archiving is only one part of a larger focus on personal heritage, which also includes hard-copy information as well as textiles and other aspects of material culture. Our involvement features our regular table of information along with a staff member available to answer questions and deliver a lecture as part of the overall program. Other collaborations have involved events in conjunction with Washington, DC–area public libraries. These activities typically involve a lecture program, along with distribution of handouts and other information.

RESULTS

Overall, I feel that our personal digital outreach activities have been very successful. While we don't have exact metrics, it's fair to say that we have brought increased awareness to many thousands of people who otherwise might have not yet heard much about the value of personal digital archiving. As awareness grows we also find that our information has been amplified through mention in major media outlets, including the *New York Times*, *Washington Post*, and *Wired*. Our guidance and related information has been citied and reposted abundantly across the Internet. Given the growing interest among the public in managing personal digital collections and given the relative novelty of outreach designed to meet the need, personal archiving outreach presents an excellent opportunity for raising an institution's profile within its community.

We have received some feedback from institutions that have used the "Personal Digital Archiving Day Kit" and are always eager to get more. To this point, the comments are positive, if a bit on the general side, such as "thank you for providing a resource we can put to use." I have no doubt that the kit can be improved, however, and hope we hear some ideas for doing so once more institutions review it and put it to use. It is quite possible, for example, that libraries, archives, and museums may have somewhat different approaches to and objectives for outreach of this type. We would like to hear about these kinds of issues so that the tool can be made more useful.

I will say that, to this point, the large majority of people we have reached have been through the Internet, principally our blog and other social media platforms. This is a function of scale and reach. Our blog gets at least 40,000 views a month; we have more than 11,000 Twitter followers; more than 5,000 people like us on Facebook. Our recorded webinars and videos on YouTube have been viewed by thousands. These counts far exceed the number of people we have been able to talk with at public events.

Beyond headcounts, it is hard to say what the impact has been. We don't know, for example, how many people have actually taken our advice to heart and tried to apply it to their own personal files. While I hope many have taken action, I actually think expanded awareness is, at this point, the main objective. Digital archiving is comparable in some sense to a public health issue connected to personal behavior. Before lots of people change their habits, they first have to hear the same message multiple times; their awareness has to rise to a certain level before the impetus for doing something different grows strong enough to result in change. At the same time as the archiving message propagates, I also believe the messenger, the Library of Congress, also benefits from a higher public profile as a provider of information that has practical bearing on people's lives.

One result that was unexpected is the willingness of a fair number of people to donate materials—digital and otherwise—to institutional collections. It seems that once people are reminded of the personal and family value of photographs and other materials, the same people recognize the potential for larger cultural value. This makes sense from a research perspective and also practically: Institutions are intended for providing enduring access to cultural heritage while individuals are not. The Library of Congress at present collects very few personal digital materials, and our outreach has not resulted in new items added to our collection. But we have referred inquirers to other institutions, and the wider potential for public donation has been demonstrated.

LESSONS LEARNED

The fundamental lesson from the Library of Congress personal digital archiving outreach is that the effort is worthwhile. We have sought to address a new and largely unknown problem and have reached thousands of people. I think that this success reflects a desire for this information, and given the explosive growth of digital information, the demand for advice will only get bigger.

Another lesson is that the guidance we developed works fairly well. When we first developed it a couple of years ago, I was prepared to revise it aggressively based on feedback. Instead, it remains largely unchanged and has been adopted by others. It can, of course, be improved but perhaps to a lesser degree than I first suspected. I also feel that the guidance is broadly suitable for other institutions to use now without much, if any, modification.

I have worked with interns and volunteers who are sometimes concerned they lack deep technical skills and worry that they don't know enough to do this kind of outreach. I assure them that, if they familiarize themselves with the guidance, they are well prepared to help people. Because most people know so little, any kind of advice adds to their knowledge. And if the issue is framed as one of basic awareness rather than complex problem solving, the pressure for those doing the outreach goes down still further. There are, of course, occasional questions that drill deeper into standards and preferred practices; they can be directed to other places, including the Library of Congress website.

It is unsurprising that we reached far more people via the Internet than through in-person events. The basic takeaway is archival outreach via social media is a highly effective use of resources. I see major value from public events, however, as they allow for deeper engagement and more personalized consideration of personal circumstances. The advice and resources packaged in our "Personal Digital Archiving Day Kit"—based on our experiences—provides a ready template that greatly simplifies holding future events.

Collaboration is well suited for personal archiving outreach. Multiple institutions can effectively leverage resources to address the collective needs of their patrons. This kind of outreach, especially if pared with eye-catching displays of obsolete technology, is also ideal as part of larger community events, such as heritage festivals, cultural awareness activities, and anniversary commemorations.

Any archiving outreach activity likely will draw questions related to digitization, and it is advisable to have some basic answers ready. But it is very important to use such questions as an opportunity to educate people on the need to look after both the analog originals and digital copies to provide for enduring access.

Any institution that undertakes this kind of outreach should also consider using it to add to community-related collections. People are open to the idea in this context, and it offers an excellent opportunity to build both collections and community connections. It seems likely that something like a "Personal Archiving and Community History Day" would have quite a bit of appeal, particularly if digital scanners (and advice for using them) were available. Staff could help select digital donations of materials that documented the local community and its cultural heritage. Something like this also should involve an appropriate technical infrastructure, including staff skills, but the bar for this is getting progressively lower.

CONCLUSION

Personally, I think personal digital archiving outreach offers some exciting and important opportunities for cultural heritage organizations. It is exciting because it gives institutions a chance to connect with communities in a new way to address a timely issue. Personal digital technology has quite a lot of cache, and outreach programs that focus on it naturally draw attention from the public and from the media. At the same time, this kind of engagement allows archivists, librarians, and other cultural heritage professionals to expand the scope of their work and demonstrate the value of their skills.

This outreach is important because focusing on personal and community digital archives will help institutions compliment their traditional holdings. As time passes, digital documentation will become increasingly valuable as a record of our times, and users will increasingly expect to find these materials among institutional holdings. Perhaps even more significant is that this outreach really makes a difference in people's lives: It helps them preserve and pass on digital memories that otherwise are at high risk of loss. While cultural professionals have always played a role in helping society at large understand the value of documentary heritage evidence, we are facing an unprecedented change in the scope and distribution of these materials, along with a steep rise in the risk of its loss. To my mind, the public service mission of librarians and archivists has never been as important or as necessary as it is now.

William LeFurgy was the digital initiatives program manager, National Digital Information and Infrastructure Program at the Library of Congress. He retired from the Library of Congress in March 2014. He is now writing on digital cultural heritage on his blog, agogified.com, and tweeting as @blefurgy.

NOTES

1. "Archive," *Merriam-Webster*, accessed September 12, 2013, http://www.merriam-webster.com/dictionary/archiving.

2. Catherine C. Marshall, "How People Manage Information over a Lifetime," in *Personal Information Management*, ed. William Jones and Jaime Teevan (Seattle: University of Washington Press, 2007), accessed September 12, 2013, http://www.csdl.tamu.edu/~marshall/PIM%20Chapter-Marshall.pdf.

3. "Personal Archiving: Preserving Your Digital Memories: Keeping Personal Digital Photographs," *Library of Congress*, accessed September 12, 2013, http://www.digitalpreservation.gov/personalarchiving/photos.html.

4. "Personal Archiving: Preserving Your Digital Memories: Overview," *Library of Congress*, accessed September 12, 2013, http://www.digitalpreservation.gov/personalarchiving.

5. "Digital Literacy," *Public Library Association*, accessed September 12, 2013, http://www.ala.org/pla/tools/digitalliteracy.

6. "Preservation Week: Pass It On," *Association for Library Collections and Technical Services*, accessed September 12, 2013, http://www.ala.org/alcts/confevents/preswk.

7. Jane Hedberg, "Preservation News," *College and Research Libraries News*, 2012, accessed September 12, 2013, http://crln.acrl.org/content/73/5/289.full.

8. "Preserving Documents and Photographs," *Kansas Historical Society*, accessed September 12, 2013, http://www.kshs.org/p/preserving-documents-photographs/12250.

9. "Digital Preservation," *Wikipedia*, accessed September 12, 2013, http://en.wikipedia.org/wiki/Digital_preservation.

10. "Digital Preservation," Library of Congress of Congress channel on *YouTube*, accessed September 12, 2013, http://www.youtube.com/playlist?list=PLEA69BE43AA9F7E68&feature=plcp.

11. "Personal Archiving Day Kit," *Library of Congress*, accessed September 12, 2013, http://www.digitalpreservation.gov/personalarchiving/padKit/index.html.

12. "The Signal: Digital Preservation," *Library of Congress*, accessed September 12, 2013, http://blogs.loc.gov/digitalpreservation.

13. National Digital Information Infrastructure and Preservation Program, *Perspectives on Personal Digital Archiving* (Washington, DC: Library of Congress, 2013), accessed September 12, 2013, http://www.digitalpreservation.gov/documents/ebookpdf_march18.pdf.

14. "Digital Preservation: National Digital Information Infrastructure and Preservation Program," *Facebook*, accessed September 12, 2013, https://www.facebook.com/digitalpreservation.

15. Heidi Glenn, "In the Digital Age, The Family Photo Album Fades Away," *NPR*, July 30, 2013, http://www.npr.org/blogs/alltechconsidered/2013/07/25/205425676/preserving-family-photos-in-digital-age.

16. Matt Baxter-Reynolds, "Personal Digital Archiving—We Need to Fix the Scale Problem," *ZDNet*, July 8, 2013, http://www.zdnet.com/personal-digital-archiving-we-need-to-fix-the-scale-problem-7000017754.

17. "ndiipp: Dispatches from the Library of Congress National Digital Information Infrastructure and Preservation Program," *Twitter*, accessed September 12, 2013, https://twitter.com/ndiipp.

18. "Preserving Your Personal Digital Memories," *Association for Library Collections and Technical Services*, accessed September 12, 2013, http://www.ala.org/alcts/confevents/upcoming/webinar/pres/042811.

Index

About the Editor

Kate Theimer is the author of the popular blog *ArchivesNext* and a frequent writer, speaker, and commentator on issues related to the future of archives. She is the author of *Web 2.0 Tools and Strategies for Archives and Local History Collections* and the editor of *A Different Kind of Web: New Connections between Archives and Our Users*, as well having contributed chapters to *Many Happy Returns: Advocacy for Archives and Archivists*, *The Future of Archives and Recordkeeping*, and the forthcoming *Encyclopedia of Archival Concepts, Principles, and Practices*. She has published articles in *The American Archivist* and the *Journal of Digital Humanities*.

Kate served on the Council of the Society of American Archivists from 2010 to 2013. Before starting her career as an independent writer and editor, she worked in the policy division of the National Archives and Records Administration in College Park, Maryland. She holds an MSI with a specialization in archives and records management from the University of Michigan and an MA in art history from the University of Maryland.